Hardanger
EMBROIDERY

The original French edition of this book was published as *Hardanger: Leçons et modèles.*

Copyright © 2013 L'inédite sarl, Paris, France, (www.editionslinedite.com).

This edition is published by arrangement with Claudia Böhme Rights & Literary Agency, Hannover, Germany (www.agency-boehme.com).

Copyright © 2014 by Stackpole Books

Published by
STACKPOLE BOOKS
5067 Ritter Road
Mechanicsburg, PA 17055
www.stackpolebooks.com

Printed in U.S.A.

10 9 8 7 6 5 4 3 2 1

First edition
Translation by Nancy Gingrich
Cover design by Wendy A. Reynolds
Interior design by Nelly Riedel

Library of Congress Cataloging-in-Publication Data

Marfaing, Fridirique, 1967?- author.
  [Hardanger. English]
  Hardanger / Fridirique Marfaing ; photography by Julien Clapot. -- First edition.
     pages cm
  "The original French edition of this book was published as Hardanger: Legons et modhles."
  ISBN 978-0-8117-1337-5
  1. Hardanger needlework. I. Clapot, Julien, illustrator. II. Title.
  TT787.M3613 2014
  746.44--dc23
                        2013041548

Hardanger
EMBROIDERY

Frédérique Marfaing

Photography by Julien Clapot

STACKPOLE
BOOKS

Contents

PROJECTS

Acknowledgments

I would like to thank the whole team at L'inédite for their remarkable work, their warm welcome, their availability, and their kindness. A special thanks to Nadia, Astrid, and Ginette. Thanks to Domi for the loan of his octagonal placemat; I know how much you have missed it!

Thanks to all my clients for their support and their faithfulness over nearly 12 years. It was a joy to share my passion for thread art with you. A special thanks to all those who trusted me enough to learn Hardanger and other drawn thread work of Cilaos with me: Dominique A., Dominique G., Odile D., Odile R., Séverine V., Monique G., Michèle B., Mireille G., Nicole L., Marine M., Denise and Dominique D., Corinne G., Caroline B., Marie-Noëlle B., Jeannine K., and all the others. The entire list from these past twelve years would be too long, but I am sure that you know who you are.

Finally, thanks to Lydia for her unconditional support for so many years . . . and to Papa, without whom all of this would have never been possible.

My thoughts also go to Michèle Brayer, who will not be able see this third volume published. We have not forgotten you.

Introduction

I discovered Hardanger embroidery in the year 2000, in a shop near Paris where I was learning to quilt. For me, it was truly love at first sight, though I didn't really start doing it until 2001, with the help of the only French book on the craft there was at the time. I was immediately captivated by it, stopping everything else—patchwork, cross stitch, traditional embroidery—and devoting all my time to Hardanger!

Wanting to share my passion, I decided to give classes at my needlework and sewing shop, *La Bobine qui Défile,* first in Villeneuve-sur-Yonne (between 2001 and 2006), then in Auxerre (from 2006 to 2012). In order to respect copyright laws and have available a teaching tool worthy of the name, I created my own designs and have already published two Hardanger books with Editions L'inédite: *L'art de broder en Hardanger* and *Broderie Hardanger.*

This third volume marks a big change in my life. On October 1, 2012, I sold my shop to explore other professional horizons. Embroidery will always remain my passion, and I hope to still find the time to provide you with new designs to enjoy. In the meantime, please enjoy my latest creations as well as some new stitches, such as the leaf. I'm hoping to hear some comments back from you!

I hope you enjoy your time embroidering the pieces you like! You are welcome to contact me at: labobinequidefile@wanadoo.fr

Frédérique Marfaing

General Tips

Hardanger embroidery (usually pronounced "har-dong-ger") is a pulled thread work embroidery of Norwegian origin, and is named after the Hardanger Fjord in southwest Norway.

Fabric

Hardanger is worked on evenweave fabric, which has the same number of threads per inch horizontally (weft) and vertically (warp).

The ideal fabric for beginners is Lugana from Zweigart. It has 25 threads per inch and is supple, and its weft is perfectly even. Its equivalent in a finer weave is Murano (32 count). You can also work with 32-count linen. Its weft is not as even, and it will therefore be a bit more difficult to embroider, but it will give superb results. Fabrics with a looser weave—from 20 to 22 threads per inch—are also suitable.

Fabric size

This book indicates the size of fabric needed for each design when using the recommended fabric. If you would like to use a tighter or looser weave, you will need to recalculate the size.

To recalculate:
- Count the number of threads (length and width) needed to make the design you have selected: for example, 150 x 90 threads.
- Count the number of threads per inch of your fabric: for example, 32 threads per inch.
- Divide the threads needed on each side by the threads per inch: $150 \div 32 = 4\frac{3}{4}$ in. and $90 \div 32 = 2\frac{3}{4}$ in.
- Add a margin of about 6 in. on each side
- This gives you get the size of fabric you need: In this example, it would be $10\frac{3}{4}$ in. x $8\frac{3}{4}$ in.

Thread and needles

The thread traditionally used for Hardanger embroidery is pearl cotton. Different sizes are used depending on the stitches and the size of the weft. This gives a certain depth to the design. You will need a size 20, 22, 24, or 26 tapestry needle, depending on the fabric and thread.

Guidelines

Here are some general guidelines for the size of thread and needles used with various types of fabric:

20-count fabric
- pearl cotton sizes 3 and 5
- needle sizes 20 and 22

25-count fabric
- pearl cotton sizes 5 and 8
- needle sizes 22 and 24

32-count fabric
- pearl cotton sizes 8 and 12
- needle sizes 24 and 26

40-count fabric
- pearl cotton size 12 and lace thread (fil à dentelle) size 80
- needle sizes 26 and 28

Scissors

You will find it easiest to work with high-quality bent embroidery scissors, such as those sold by Prym. They are very thin and very pointed, and therefore very fragile, but they will make cutting and removing threads much easier.

Embroidery hoop

Whether or not to use an embroidery hoop is up to you. Try it with and without. However, a hoop does help to stretch the fabric so that you can easily count the threads. In addition, using a hoop will help keep your work more even.

I prefer to use a 6"-diameter hoop for working satin stitch and a 4¾" hoop for all other stitches, even with larger projects. This allows me to be closer to the stitch in order to achieve the best possible result. I remove the hoop to make blanket stitch borders and the Scandinavian four-sided stitch, but it this is not necessary. The most important thing is to to work in a way that feels comfortable to you.

Always remove your hoop when you are not embroidering to keep it from leaving too much of a mark on the fabric.

Reading diagrams

In Hardanger, unlike cross-stitch, you must count threads, not holes. You must therefore count the number of lines in the diagram.

One line corresponds to one thread of weft or warp.

The empty spaces show where threads will be removed.

Always start with the center of the work and count the number of threads needed to the closest motif.

In the beginning, reading the diagrams may seem difficult. Use the keys and refer to the corresponding lessons to make the stitches.

Colors

Your choice of colors is important, as the outcome depends on it. Hardanger is traditionally embroidered tone on tone, either white on white or ivory on ivory. Dare to try working with different colors; the results may surprise you and your eyes will thank you! When browsing through this book, don't fixate on the colors shown, thinking, "I don't like this design because I hate red." Change the color or embroider tone on tone and you may find you love the design after all.

Starting your work

Begin by selecting your fabric and thread. Be careful to match the thickness of your thread to your choice of fabric. If you change either of them from what is recommended in the pattern, refer to the information on page 8 to make sure you have appropriate sizes of both.

Cut your fabric to the size required. Begin by pulling a thread out along the whole length of the fabric (near the edge) and cut along the space created; then you will have a straight line. Finish the edges of the fabric with an overcast stitch to prevent fraying.

Fold your fabric in half both ways to find the center and start there. You may wish to put in basting lines to help with counting threads when stitching. Work the satin stitches of each block first, then cut and remove threads, and finally add the weaving and filling stitches inside the block.

Be aware that Hardanger is a geometric embroidery. If you make any mistake at all, you will not be able to cut the opening. So, some advice: Count often! Check all the time to see if your satin stitches are facing each other by sliding the needle from one stitch to the next. When you have finished a diamond, it must be closed. If it is not, look for the mistake and start over; don't cut the opening!

Securing the end of the thread

Finish off your thread on the wrong side of the fabric, of course! Secure the thread by slipping the needle and thread under several stitches, blocks of satin stitches, or bars. Never make a knot.

Washing

When your design is finished, don't be afraid to wash it. A basin of warm water and a mild detergent will do the trick. Leave it to soak a bit, then rinse, and iron while damp.

However, if you use a brightly-colored fabric (such as bright or dark red), soak it first, before embroidering it, to be sure the color will not bleed. If it does, change the water often, until it remains clear. You can also add vinegar or coarse salt to stabilize the color.

Lesson 1:
Satin Stitch (Kloster Blocks) and Variations

Instructions

A – Kloster (Satin Stitch) Blocks

Use pearl cotton size 5 for 25 ct fabric or size 8 for 32 ct fabric. Kloster blocks always consist of five stitches worked over four threads of the fabric.

Whenever possible, work from the outside towards the inside as follows:
- bring the needle up at 1
- insert it at 2,
- bring it up again at 3,
- insert it at 4, etc.

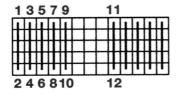

When you have inserted the needle at 2, never bring it up at 4. The needle must always be brought up on the opposite side, at 3, to avoid problems when the fabric threads are cut.

To move from one block to the next, proceed as indicated on the diagram—insert the needle at 10 and bring it up at 11—so the back side will also look neat.

Making diagonals (used in diamond shapes, for example) involves alternating vertical and horizontal kloster blocks.

For a neat reverse side, move from a vertical block to a horizontal block as follows:
- come up at 3,
- insert needle at 4,
- come up at 5,
- insert needle at 4.

To move from a horizontal block to a vertical block:
- come up at 7,
- insert needle at 6,
- come up at 7,
- insert needle at 8.

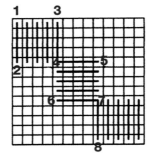

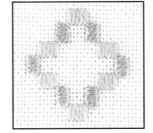

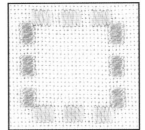

B – Norwegian Star

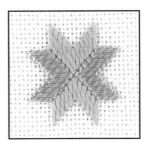

This motif is one of numerous variations of the satin stitch. You will discover others when embroidering the mini cushions (p. 66).

Use pearl cotton size 5 for 25 ct fabric or pearl cotton size 8 for 32 ct fabric and embroider from the outside toward the inside. Then work following the numbers.

Each stitch covers 6 threads and shifts down or up from the previous stitch by one thread.

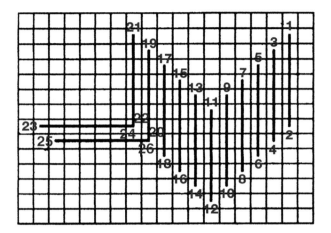

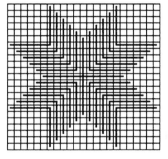

C – Tulip motif

This motif is one of the numerous variations of the satin stitch. You will discover others when embroidering the mini cushions (p. 66).

Use pearl cotton size 5 for 25 ct fabric or pearl cotton size 8 for 32 ct fabric and embroider from the outside toward the inside. Make stitches following the numbers and increasing or decreasing the stitch length as shown in the diagram.

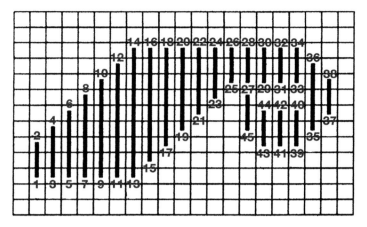

Work the second half of the motif—or more, if needed—in the same way.

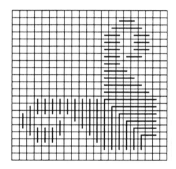

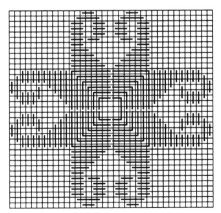

Lesson 2:
Cutting and Removing Threads

Instructions

A – Cutting threads in small squares

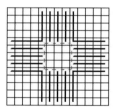

In the diagram below, the threads to be cut are indicated by the dotted lines. Always cut vertically, slightly lifting the thread to cut it very close to the base of the block.

Cut the 4 threads carefully, one at a time, next to the edge of the satin stitches. Turn the work and proceed in the same manner for the other three sides of the square.

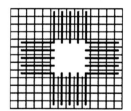

B – Cutting and removing threads in squares and diamonds

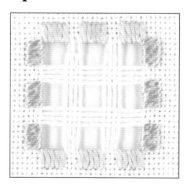

In the diagrams below, the threads to be cut are indicated by the dotted lines. The principle remains the same regardless of the shape or size of the motif. Always cut vertically, lifting the thread up slightly to cut it close to the edge of the satin stitches.

Cut the first 4 threads carefully, one at a time, next to the edge of the satin stitches. Leave the next 4, cut the following 4, and so on.

Continue in the same manner with the threads on the opposite side. Use tweezers to pull the threads out. Then repeat on the two remaining edges.

Cutting and removing threads from squares

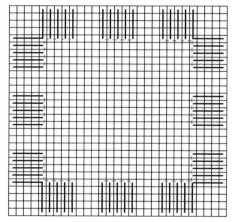

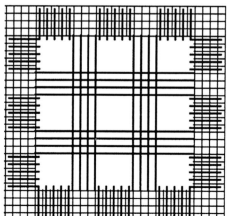

Cutting and removing threads from diamonds

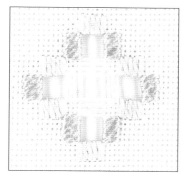

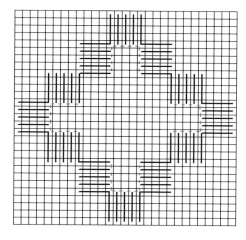

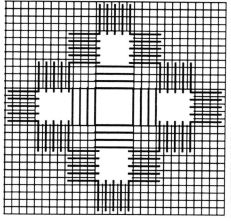

A little trick!

Even when you cut as closely as possible with the best pair of scissors possible, there will always be little tufts of threads on the edge.

When the embroidery is done tone on tone, these tufts aren't very noticeable. However, when the embroidery is in color, they look very unsightly!

Here is how to make these threads disappear:
- First, cut following the direction of the weft: 2 threads on the right side of the work, and 2 threads on the wrong side;
- Second, tuck the little remaining tufts under the satin stitch using your embroidery needle. Always follow the direction of the weft and put the little threads back under on the side where they come up, either on the right side or on the wrong side.

Lesson 3:
Wrapped (Overcast) Bars

Instructions

Work the kloster blocks, then cut and remove the threads to produce the open spaces. Use pearl cotton size 8 for 25 ct fabric or size 12 for 32 ct fabric.

This stitch consists of wrapping the embroidery thread around the remaining weft or warp fabric threads. It is important to pull the threads together tightly and to make sure all the stitches lie right next to each other without overlapping.

To progress from one bar to the next, move from behind the completed bar either across in a straight line or diagonally at right angles, for a neat back side and an attractive bar. It is very difficult, if not impossible, to secure the end of your embroidery thread under a wrapped bar. Therefore, make sure your thread is long enough to be able to reach the edge so you can secure the end of the thread under the satin stitches.

A – Wrapped bars over 4 threads

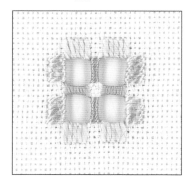

B – Wrapped bars over 2 threads

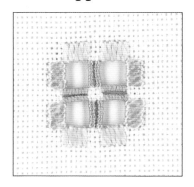

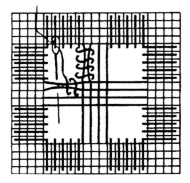

Lesson 4:
Woven Bars

Instructions

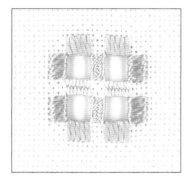

Work the kloster blocks, then cut and remove the threads to produce the open spaces. Use pearl cotton size 8 for 25 ct fabric or size 12 for 32 ct fabric.

For woven bars, bring your needle up in the middle of 4 fabric (weft) threads at the edge of the work (at 1 on the diagram). Position your fabric so the bar you are working on lies horizontally, then make a figure eight with the embroidery thread as follows:
• bring the needle over the 2 upper weft threads,
• take the needle back under these same threads,
• bring the needle up and over the 2 lower weft threads,
• take the needle back under these same threads.

Continue in the same manner.

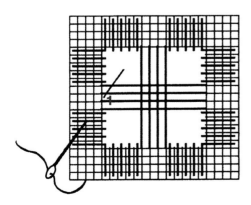

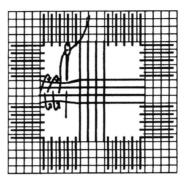

To progress from one bar to the next, it is best to move diagonally at right angles to keep the back side neat.

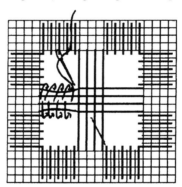

Lesson 5:
Uneven Woven Bars

Instructions

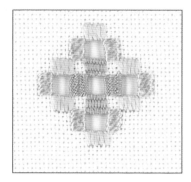

Complete the kloster blocks, then cut and remove the threads.

Use pearl cotton size 8 for 25 ct fabric and pearl cotton size 12 for 32 ct fabric.

This is also a woven stitch. Start by placing your needle and thread:
• under the first fabric thread,
• then over the next two fabric threads,
• then under the fourth fabric thread.

Going back:
• bring the needle up and over the fourth fabric thread,
• then under the next 2 threads
• then over the first thread.

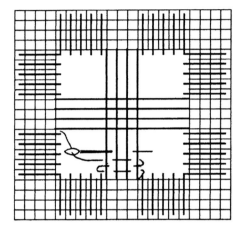

When moving on to another bar, work diagonally at right angles to keep the back side neat.

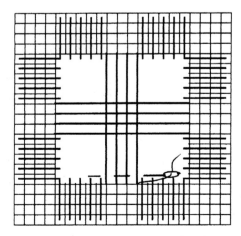

Lesson 6:
Eyelet Stitch and Variations

All three of these stitches are basically the same. In fact, they are a family of stitches that change only in length or spacing.

Instructions

A – Star Stitch (Algerian Eye)

Use pearl cotton size 8 for 25 ct fabric or pearl cotton size 12 for 32 ct fabric.

Make this stitch by repeatedly bringing the needle up from the outside edge and inserting it in the same central point, leaving 2 fabric threads between each pair of stitches on the outside edge.

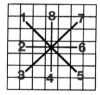 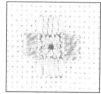

B – Eyelet Stitch

Use pearl cotton size 8 for 25 ct fabric or pearl cotton size 12 for 32 ct fabric.

Embroider from the outside towards the inside, inserting the needle in the same central point each time and leaving only one fabric thread between each pair of stitches on the outside edge.

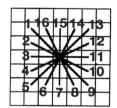 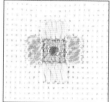

C – Madeira Star

Use pearl cotton size 8 for 25 ct fabric or pearl cotton size 12 for 32 ct fabric.

This stitch is identical to the star stitch, with only the length of the stitches changing. Each stitch is made over four fabric threads.

Make this stitch by repeatedly bringing the needle up from the outside edge and inserting it in the same central point, leaving 2 fabric threads between each pair of stitches on the outside edge.

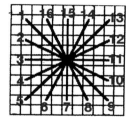 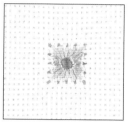

Lesson 7:
Loop Stitches

Instructions

A – Dove's Eye Filling Stitch (Straight Loop Stitch) in Kloster Blocks

Use pearl cotton size 8 for 25 ct fabric or pearl cotton size 12 for 32 ct fabric. After embroidering the kloster blocks, cut and remove the threads. Work the dove's eye stitch as shown below.

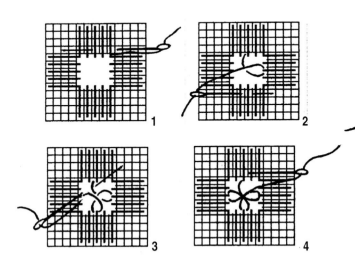

B – Dove's Eye Filling Stitch (Straight Loop Stitch) in Woven Bars

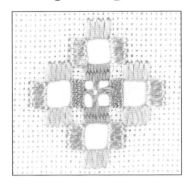

Use pearl cotton size 8 for 25 ct fabric or pearl cotton size 12 for 32 ct fabric.

Start by working the kloster blocks and cutting and removing the threads. Work three and a half of the woven bars around the space for the stitch.

Start the dove's eye stitch in the middle of the last bar, stitching as shown below:

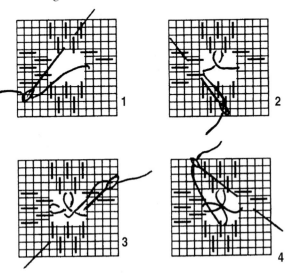

After returning to the starting point, finish weaving the last half of the bar.

C – Square Filet Filling Stitch
(Oblique Loop Stitch)

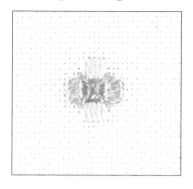

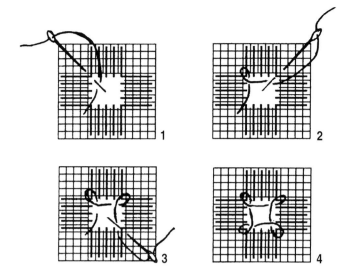

Work the kloster blocks or the woven bars, then cut and remove the threads.

Next, with pearl cotton size 8 for 25 ct fabric or pearl cotton size 12 for 32 ct fabric, stitch as shown at right.

Lesson 8:
Picots

Instructions

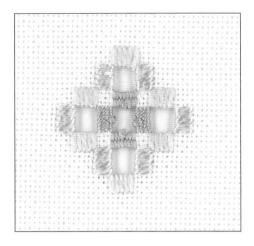

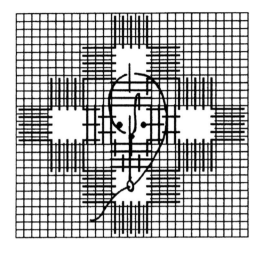

Complete the kloster blocks and cut and remove the threads.

Then, with pearl cotton size 8 for 25 ct fabric or size 12 for 32 ct fabric, work half a woven bar.

Bring the needle up vertically in the middle of the 4 threads, with the eye of the needle pointing towards you.

Make sure the loop formed goes under both the eye and the top of the needle, as shown.

Pull the needle toward you; the knot thus made will form the first picot.

Finish working the remainder of the bar.

You can make a larger picot by wrapping the embroidery thread around the needle once more.

Lesson 9:
Buttonhole Stitch

Instructions

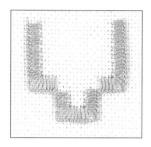

Use pearl cotton size 8 for 25 ct fabric or size 12 for 32 ct fabric.

A – Buttonhole stitch worked in straight rows

This edging is stitched over 4 threads, with the point of the needle always facing you. Work as follows:

* bring the needle up at the edge of the border, (at point 1),
* insert it 4 threads back (point 2),
* bring it up at 3, keeping the embroidery thread under the needle, then pull;
* insert the needle one space over and 4 threads back (point 4),
* bring it up at 5, keeping the embroidery thread under the needle, then pull.

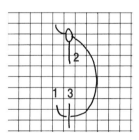

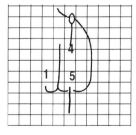

Continue in this pattern along the border.

Keeping the embroidery thread under the needle makes a gently curved ridge that forms the edge.

B – Buttonhole stitch worked diagonally at right angles

There are two different ways to turn a corner.

You can turn an inner corner as follows:
* insert needle at 1,
* come up at 2,
* insert needle at 3,
* come up at 2,
* insert needle at 4,
* come up at 5.

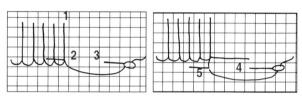

For an outer corner, turn the second way:
* insert needle again at the same point 1,
* come up at 2,
* insert needle at 1,
* come up at 3, with 2 threads between stitches;

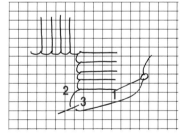

- insert needle at 1,
- come up at 4, with 2 threads between stitches,
- insert needle at 1,
- come up at 5, with 2 threads between stitches, turning to make the right angle;

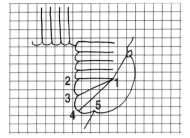

- insert needle at 1,
- come up at 6, with 2 threads between stitches.

The embroidery thread is again straight over 4 fabric threads.

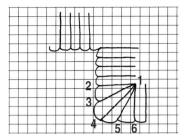

When you finish embroidering the buttonhole stitches, cut the fabric as close to the outside embroidered edge as possible, along the little ridge formed by the stitches. Feel free to place a bit of fabric glue along your stitches to ensure that the buttonhole edge remains firm.

Lesson 10:
Scandinavian Four-Sided Stitch

Instructions

A – Four-sided stitch

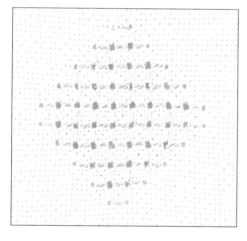

Use pearl cotton size 5, 8, or 12, depending on the desired effect and the fabric used.

To make this stitch, embroider a cross on the back to obtain a square the width of four fabric threads on the right side. To do this, follow the diagram below:
• bring needle up at 1, then insert at 2;
• bring needle up at 3, insert at 1;
• bring needle up at 4, insert at 2;
• bring needle up at 3, insert at 4;
• bring needle up at 5, insert at 3;
• bring needle up at 6, insert at 4;
• bring needle up at 5, insert at 6, etc.

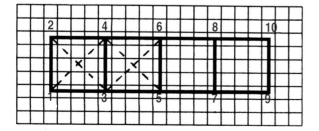

B – Drawn thread work band

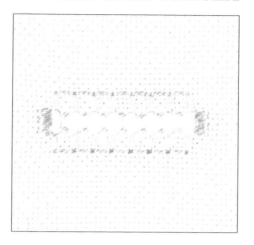

Use pearl cotton size 5, 8, or 12, depending on the desired effect and the fabric used.

To make this drawn thread band, the steps are the same as for the previous block, except that you are working four-sided stitches on both sides of an area where 4 fabric threads (or more, depending on the pattern) have been removed. This allows the remaining threads (in this case, vertical) to be pulled together in groups of 4 threads as the sides of the band are embroidered.

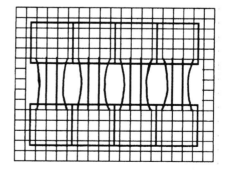

C – Four-sided edging stitch

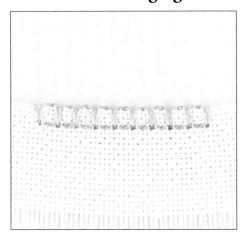

Use pearl cotton size 8 for 25 ct fabric or size 12 for 32 ct fabric.

This stitch is worked in 2 steps:

Backstitch over 4 threads, going over each stitch a second time before moving on to the next stitch. Work as follows:
• bring the needle up at A and insert at B,
• come up again at A and insert again at B,
• bring needle up at C and insert at A,
• come up again at C and insert again at A,
• bring needle up at D and insert at C.

Continue in the same manner along the edge of the piece of embroidery. Tighten the thread slightly to create a lacy appearance when the edging is completed.

When you have gone all the way around with the double backstitch, fold the outside edge of the fabric under at the line of backstitching, folding it under a little bit at a time as you complete the second step of this edging stitch.

Continue to make stitches over 4 fabric threads, in the following manner:
• bring needle up at A and bring over folded band at B,
• come up again through the 2 thicknesses of fabric at A,
• bring the needle over folded band again to B,
• from the back side, insert the needle 4 fabric threads to the side to come up at C,
• make a backstitch from C to A on the right side and then from A to C on the wrong side and bring the needle up again at C,
• bring the needle over the top of the folded band to D and begin again, working in the same manner around the edge.

For the corners, make the stitch in the same way; there will be 4 thicknesses of fabric, which makes the work a bit more difficult but does not change the pattern.

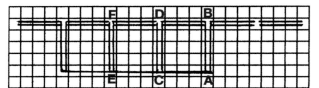

When the edging is completed, pull out 1 or 2 fabric threads on the wrong side along the stitching to make it easier to trim off the excess fabric.

Lesson 11:
Cross Stitch

Instructions

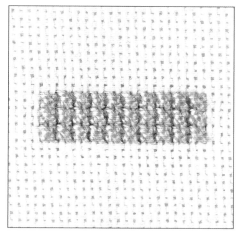

Use 2 strands of cotton embroidery floss.

Make a cross stitch over 2 fabric threads. This is done in 2 steps.

First, make one half of each cross stitch along the entire row:
• bring the needle up at 1, insert at 2,
• bring the needle up at 3, insert at 4, etc.

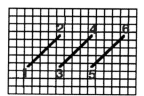

Complete the second half of the crosses in the reverse direction:
• bring the needle up at 7, insert at 8,
• bring the needle up at 9, insert at 10, etc.

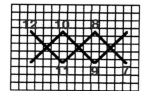

Lesson 12:
Twisted Lattice Band

Instructions

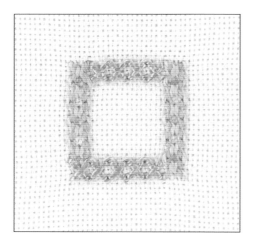

Use pearl cotton size 5 for 25 ct fabric or pearl cotton size 8 for 32 ct fabric.

Make a cross stitch over 4 fabric threads. This is done in two steps. Make one half of each cross stitch along the entire row (diagram 1), then complete the second half of the crosses in the reverse direction (diagram 2):
• bring the needle up at 1, insert at 2,
• bring the needle up at 3, insert at 4,
• bring the needle up at 5, insert at 6.

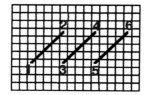

And on the way back:
• bring the needle up at 7, insert at 8,
• bring the needle up at 9, insert at 10,
• bring the needle up at 11, insert at 12.

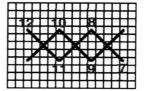

Next, weave through the cross stitches. Begin on the lower edge, stitching from left to right.

Bring the needle up at the base of the cross and work as follows:
• slide the embroidery thread under the bottom left quarter of the cross stitch,
• pass it over the center of the cross,
• then slide the needle under the bottom right quarter of the cross,
• and bring it again over the base of the cross before sliding it under the bottom left quarter of the next cross stitch.

Continue in this pattern to the end of the row and then return, weaving through the top edge in the same manner.

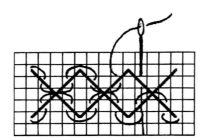

Lesson 13:
Variations on the Cable Stitch

Instructions
Depending on the desired effect and the thickness of the fabric, embroider with pearl cotton size 5, 8, or 12.

A – Horizontal double cable stitch

This stitch is made over 4 fabric threads, with a space of two fabric threads between the 2 rows. These rows are completed at the same time as follows:
• bring the embroidery thread up at 1,
• insert the needle at 2,
• bring up the needle at 3,

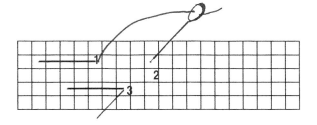

• draw the embroidery thread through (1 in the diagram below),
• insert the needle at 2,
• bring up the needle at 3.

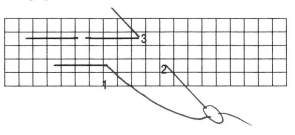

It will look like this:

B – Horizontal triple cable stitch

This stitch is made in 2 steps. Embroider a horizontal double cable as shown above, then stitch a second series of double cable stitches, overlapping one side of the first one, which will become the center line:

- bring the embroidery thread through at 1,
- insert the needle at 2,
- bring up the needle at 3.

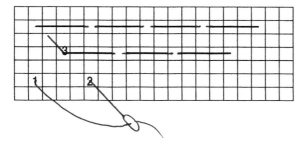

- pull the embroidery thread through at 1,
- insert the needle at 2,
- bring up the needle at 3.

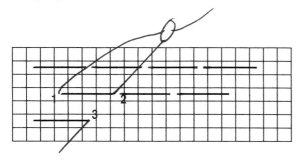

The row of double cable stitches will look like this:

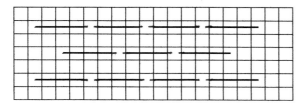

C – Turning corners
A backstitch is used to turn a corner. To do this:
- bring the embroidery thread up at 1,
- insert the needle at 2,
- bring up the needle at 3,

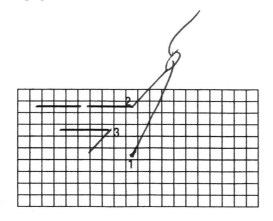

- bring the embroidery thread up at 1,
- insert the needle at 2,
- bring up the needle at 3.

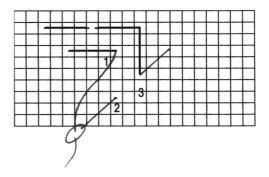

It will look like this:

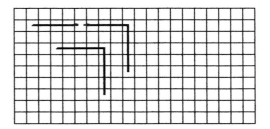

D – Diagonal double cable stitch

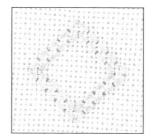

The principle here is pretty much the same as for the horizontal double cable stitch. However, the stitches are made over 2 fabric threads and are spaced 2 threads apart. To work this stitch:
- bring the needle up at 1,
- insert the needle at 2,
- bring the needle up at 3,

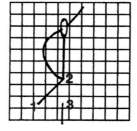

- insert the needle at 4,
- bring it up at 2,

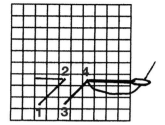

- insert the needle at 5,
- bring it up at 4, etc.

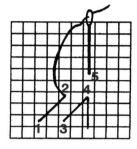

E – Diagonal triple cable stitch

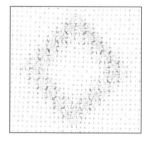

This stitch is made in 2 steps. Embroider a diagonal double cable as shown above, then stitch a second series of double cable stitches, overlapping one side of the first one, which will become the center line.

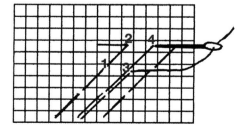

A backstitch is used to turn the corner. Follow the diagram below:
- bring the needle up at 1,
- insert the needle at 2,
- bring it up at 3,

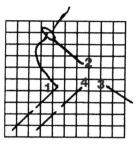

- insert the needle at 2,
- bring it up at 4,

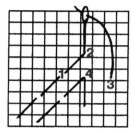

- insert the needle at 5,
- bring it up at 3, etc.

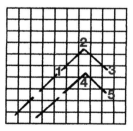

F – Backstitch
Work over 2 fabric threads as indicated below:

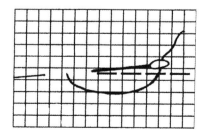

Lesson 14:
Greek Cross

Instructions

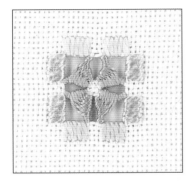

Work the kloster blocks, then cut and remove the threads.

Use pearl cotton size 8 for 25 ct fabric or size 12 for 32 ct fabric.

Make wrapped bar A over 2 fabric threads, working from the outside towards the center. Then bring the needle up at 1, which is the angle between A and the 2 threads marked C.

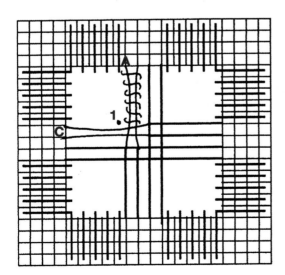

Interweave bar A and the 2 threads C, working as follows:
• with the embroidery thread at 1,
• take it over the 2 threads C,
• bring the needle under those same threads, and then up again at point 1,

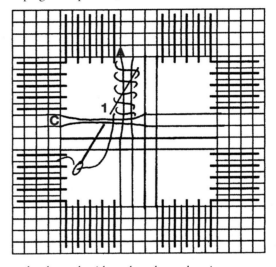

• take the embroidery thread over bar A,
• bring the needle back under that bar, and then up again at point 1,
• continue in the same manner.

Stop this stitch in the middle of the bars and finish wrapped bar C over 2 threads. Complete the other 3 arms of the cross in the same manner.

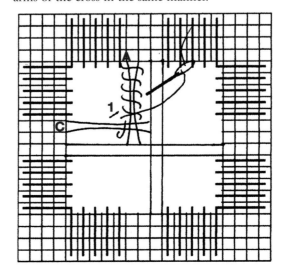

Lesson 15:
Diagonal Twisted Bars

Instructions

A – Diagonal twisted bars or wrapped bars

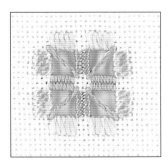

Work the kloster blocks, then cut and remove the threads.

Use pearl cotton size 8 for 25 ct fabric or pearl cotton size 12 for 32 ct fabric.

Make the woven bars or wrapped bars, following the design.

To make the diagonal twisted bars, insert a thread from the outside corner to the center, from A to B.

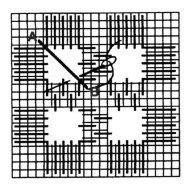

Then bring the thread back to the starting point, twisting it around the length of the diagonal thread 2 or 3 times.

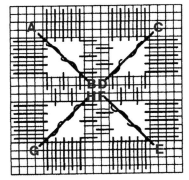

Make the 3 other diagonal bars in the same way:
• from C to D,
• from E to F,
• and from G to H.

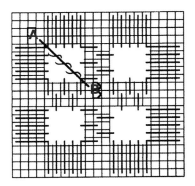

The bars can meet in the center of the motif as well, and in this case the stitches are completed as above, working:

• from A to B,
• from C to B,
• from D to B,
• and from E to B.

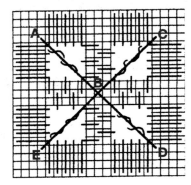

This type of bar is frequently used to form more elaborate stitches and is therefore often embroidered over.

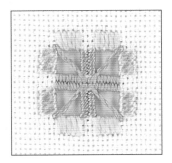

B – Diagonal twisted bars with center rosette (spider's web filling stitch)

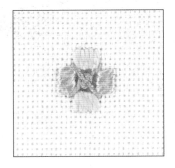

Work the kloster blocks, then cut and remove the threads.

Use pearl cotton size 8 for 25 ct fabric or pearl cotton size 12 for 32 ct fabric.

Take your thread diagonally from A to B and then bring it back to the starting point, wrapping it around the length of the diagonal thread two times.

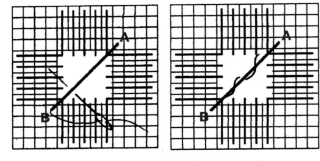

Slide the embroidery thread under the satin stitches to get to point C.

Take the thread diagonally from C to D and then bring it back halfway, wrapping it just once around the diagonal thread to the intersection with the opposite thread.

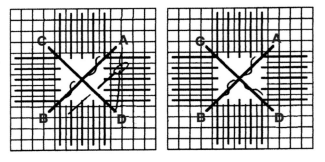

To make the center rosette, or web, weave over and under the bars, forming a circle. Go around 2 times.

Finish by wrapping the thread once around the second half of bar CD.

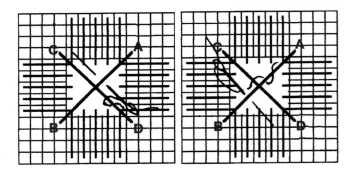

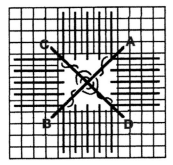

Lesson 16:
Divided Branch (Crow's Foot) Stitch

Instructions

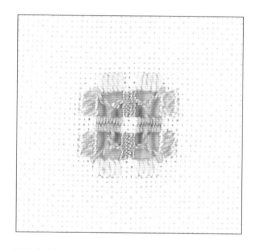

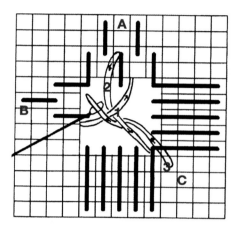

Work kloster blocks, then cut and remove the threads.

Use pearl cotton size 8 for 25 ct fabric or pearl cotton size 12 for 32 ct fabric.

Make woven bar A and weave half of bar B.

Begin the divided branch stitch in the middle of bar B and work as follows:
• insert needle from back into the middle of bar A,
• bring needle up at A and then carry thread to opposite corner C and insert needle from the back,
• bring the needle up at corner C,
• take thread 3 under thread 2 then over thread 1,
• return to the middle of bar B,
• finish weaving on last half of bar B.

Lesson 17:
Single Ringed Backstitch

Instructions

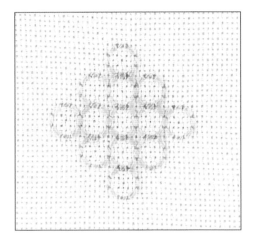

Use pearl cotton size 8 for 25 ct fabric or pearl cotton size 12 for 32 ct fabric.

Embroider in 2 steps.

Backstitch over 2 fabric threads as indicated below, forming a "wave" pattern from one end of the row to the other.

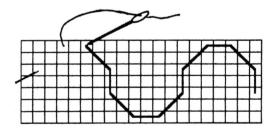

Return, making the same "wave" pattern as above on the other half of the row, to form octagonal shapes.

Each time the 2 waves meet, the threads are on top of each other, which will give some depth to the design as some stitches will be single and others double.

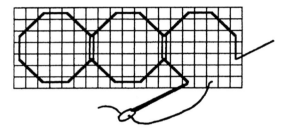

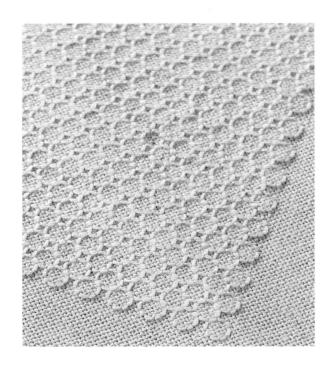

Lesson 18:
Rosette Stitch

Instructions

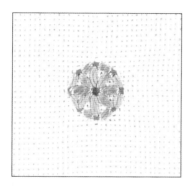

Use pearl cotton size 8 for 25 ct fabric or pearl cotton size 12 for 32 ct fabric.

Embroider using straight stitch, going over each stitch twice, and pulling on the thread to accentuate the openings.

Make the inside stitches first, following the numbers and always inserting the needle down into the center.

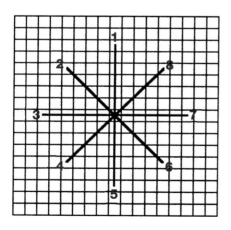

After that, work the outside circle in backstitch, following the order of the letters.

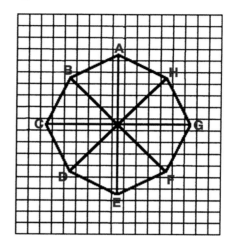

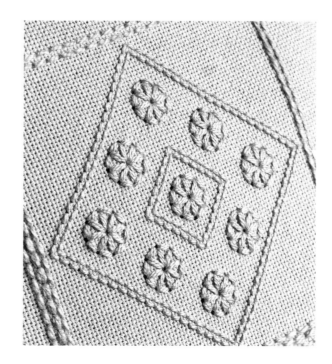

Lesson 19:
Laticework

Instructions

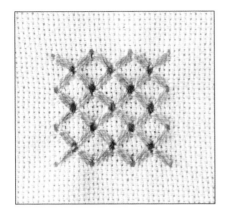

Work kloster blocks, if necessary.

Use pearl cotton size 5 for 25 ct fabric or pearl cotton size 8 for 32 ct fabric.

Complete this stitch as follows, pulling tightly on the thread in order to obtain openings at each intersection.

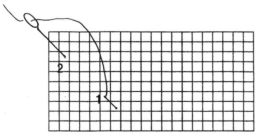

Bring the needle up at 1, insert at 2, bring it up at 1.

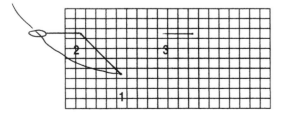

Bring the needle up at 1, insert at 2, bring it up at 3 (8 fabric threads to the right of 2).

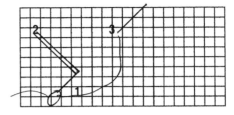

Bring the needle up at 3, insert at 1, bring it up again at 3. Repeat this step a second time.

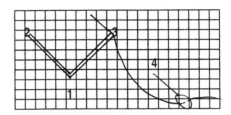

Bring the needle up at 3, insert at 4, bring it up at 3.

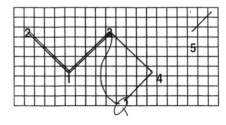

Bring the needle up at 3, insert at 4, bring it up at 5.

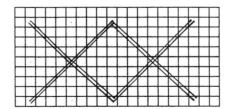

The finished embroidery (with two rows of diagonal stitches) will look like this.

Lesson 20:
Fly Stitch

Instructions

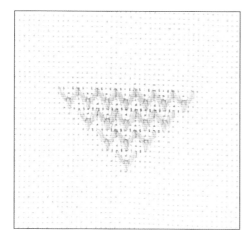

Use pearl cotton size 5 for 25 ct fabric or pearl cotton size 8 for 32 ct fabric. Work as follows:

- bring the needle up at A,
- insert at C,
- bring it up at D, being careful to have the needle go over the working thread.

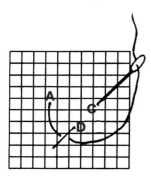

Continue by inserting the needle at E.

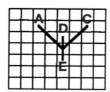

This is what the finished stitch will look like:

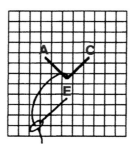

Repeat these steps horizontally or vertically as indicated in the design.

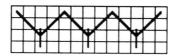

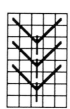

Lesson 21: Woven Inset

Instructions

Embroider the kloster blocks, then cut and remove the threads as needed.

Use pearl cotton size 8 for 25 ct fabric or pearl cotton size 12 for 32 ct fabric.

Make woven bars as indicated in the design, then work the diagonal crosses as follows: stitch diagonally from A to B, then return from B to A; repeat this step once. You should have 4 diagonal threads in all.

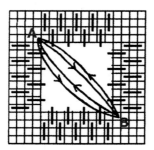

Continue in the same manner from C to D, being careful to cross these threads to form a weft with those just made in the opposite direction.

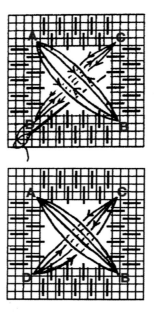

Weave through these diagonal threads as with woven bars.

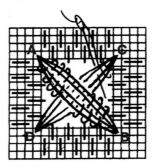

When all 4 crosses are completed, make a central wheel or web by weaving over and under the spokes formed by the bars and the diagonals in the 4 squares.

Weave around 4 or 5 times, using pearl cotton size 5 for 25 ct fabric or pearl cotton size 8 for 32 ct fabric.

Lesson 22: Woven Petals

Instructions

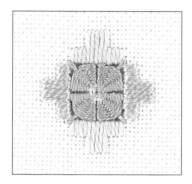

Use pearl cotton size 8 for 25 ct fabric or size 12 for 32 ct fabric.

Work the kloster blocks, then cut and remove the threads.

Note: Do not embroider the bars.

Make the diagonal twisted bars (see Lesson 15).

Then, start from the center of the motif in the middle of one of the bars at point A.

Weave the embroidery thread:
• over the bar,
• under the diagonal twisted bar,
• over the outside two fabric threads of the next bar.

Return back to A, taking the needle:
• under those two fabric threads of the bar,
• over the diagonal twisted bar,
• under the two fabric threads of the first bar.

Continue in the same manner until the end of the bar.

Return to the center of the motif by sliding the embroidery thread under the woven petal.

Complete the other three petals in the same manner.

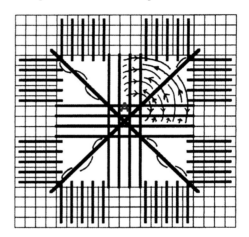

Lesson 23: Ribbed Wheel (Backstitched Spider's Web)

Instructions

Work the kloster blocks, then cut and remove the threads. Use pearl cotton size 8 for 25 ct fabric or pearl cotton size 12 for 32 ct fabric.

Work wrapped bars over 4 fabric threads to form the main cross (see Lesson 3).

Make diagonal twisted bars (see Lesson 15) by inserting the embroidery thread diagonally from the outside corner to the middle, and then returning to the outside, twisting the thread twice around the first thread. Do the same with the other 3 corners.

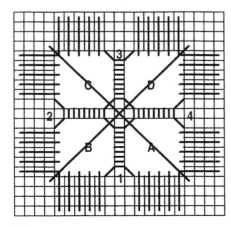

To make this motif, work in backstitch, starting from the center of the motif. To do this:
- take the embroidery thread around twisted bar A, then under bar 1,
- take the embroidery thread around bar 1, then under twisted bar B.

Keep the tension on the thread tight by pulling gently on it after every wrap. The last diagram shows what it should look like after several times around.

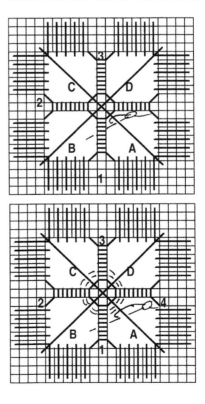

Continue to work in this manner around the 8 bars until the wrapped bars are completely covered.

This motif is often used to embellish the corners of pulled thread work. In such instances, it is impossible to make wrapped bars, so it will be necessary to substitute twisted bars.

Lesson 24:
Four-Petal Flower (¾ Spider Web)

Instructions

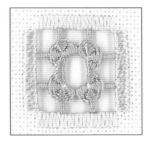

Make a square with 21 satin stitches on each side.

Then cut and remove threads on each side as follows: cut 5 threads, leave 2 threads, cut 6 threads, leave 2 threads, and cut 5 threads.

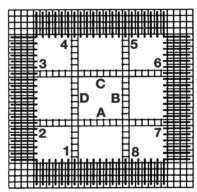

Use pearl cotton size 8 for 25 ct fabric or size 12 for 32 ct fabric. Make wrapped bars over 2 fabric threads for bars 1 to 8 first, then bar B.

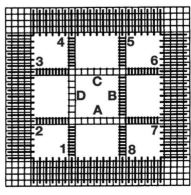

At the end of bar B, make the first petal.

For this stitch, take the embroidery thread:
• over bar C, under 5, over 6, and under B.

Then turn to go back:
• over bar B, under 6, over 5, under C.

Continue in this manner until the petal covers half of bars B and C. Finish wrapping bar C before moving on to the next petal.

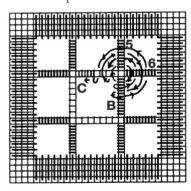

Make the 3 other petals in the same manner. When the motif is completed, secure the embroidery thread under the petals.

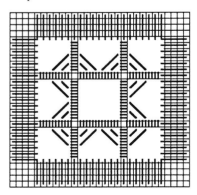

You may wish to add a dove's eye in the center of the motif to form the heart of the flower.

Lesson 25:
Fan Stitch
(Woven Triple Spokes)

Instructions

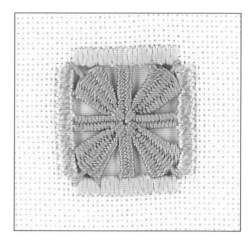

Make a square with 21 satin stitches on each side, then cut and remove threads as follows: cut 8 threads, leave 4 threads, then cut the next 8 threads.

Use pearl cotton size 8 for 25 ct fabric or pearl cotton size 12 for 32 ct fabric.

Work woven bars over the 4 threads left (see Lesson 4).

Then make three diagonal twisted bars (see Lesson 15) from each corner to the center, wrapping the thread around the bar 3 times as you bring it back:
• 1 starting at the corner,
• 1 to its right, 5 satin stitches from the corner,
• 1 to its left, 5 satin stitches from the corner.

Next, starting from the center of the motif, in the middle of bar A, weave through these 3 twisted thread spokes.

Bring the embroidery thread:
• over the first twisted spoke,
• under the second twisted spoke,
• over the third twisted spoke.

Then return, going:
• under the third twisted spoke,
• over the second twisted spoke,
• under the first twisted spoke.

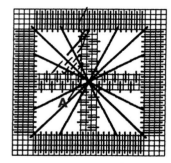

The center is tight and the motif widens as it goes out, resembling a fan.

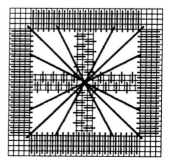

Lesson 26:
Spider

Instructions

A – Openwork spider

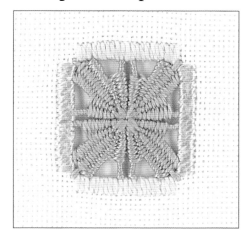

Make a square with 21 satin stitches on each side, then cut and remove threads as follows: cut 8 threads, leave 4, then cut the next 8 threads.

Use pearl cotton size 8 for 25 ct fabric or pearl cotton size 12 for 32 ct fabric.

With the 4 remaining threads, work sets of divided wrapped bars over 2 threads each (see Lesson 3).

Then make three diagonal twisted bars (see Lesson 15) from each corner to the center, twisting the thread around the diagonal thread 3 times as you bring it back:
• 1 starting at the corner,
• 1 to its right between the third and fourth satin stitches,
• 1 to its left between the third and fourth satin stitches.

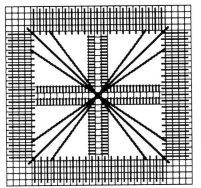

Next, starting from the center of the motif, between two wrapped bars, weave through the 5 spokes of one of the corners, (the 3 twisted diagonal thread spokes and the 2 wrapped bars on either side of the spokes).

Take the embroidery thread:
• over the wrapped bar,
• under the first twisted spoke,
• over the second twisted spoke,
• under the third twisted spoke,
• and over the wrapped bar.

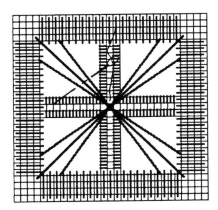

Then turn to go back:
• under the wrapped bar,
• over the third twisted spoke,
• under the second twisted spoke,
• over the first twisted spoke,
• and under the wrapped bar.

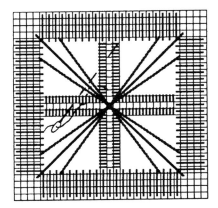

A bit more than halfway up the bar, continue in this same manner, but only over the three twisted spokes in the center. Go all the way to the edge in this manner.

Do the same with the other three corners.

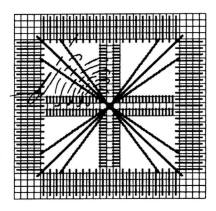

B – Spider without openwork

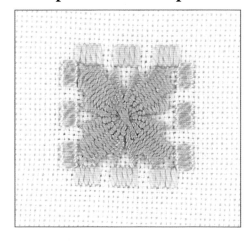

Work kloster blocks as indicated in the diagram. Use pearl cotton size 8 for 25 ct fabric or pearl cotton size 12 for 32 ct fabric. Without cutting and removing any threads, make embroidery thread spokes as indicated in the diagram:
• come up at 1,
• insert at 2,
• come up at 3,
• insert at 4, and continue in the same manner through number 20.

The dotted lines indicate where the thread goes on the back side of the work.

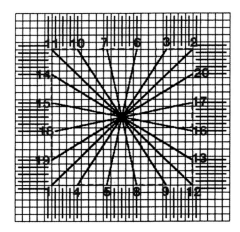

Starting from the center of the spokes of thread, embroider a ribbed wheel (see Lesson 23). The embroidery thread must go around each of the spokes of thread.

Go around the wheel three times.

Then, as in section A, finish the spider by weaving first over and under the 5 threads of one of the corners, then over and under the 3 central threads (still without going through the fabric).

Complete the other three corners in the same manner.

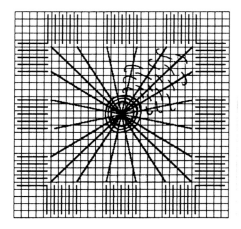

Lesson 27: Edelweiss

Instructions

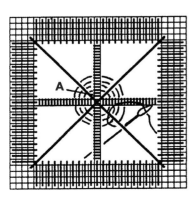

Work a square with 21 satin stitches on each side, then cut and remove threads as follows: cut 9 threads, leave 2, then cut the next 9 threads.

Use pearl cotton size 8 for 25 ct fabric or size 12 for 32 ct fabric.

Make wrapped bars over the two remaining fabric threads (see Lesson 3).

Then make diagonal twisted bars from each corner to the center (see Lesson 15), twisting the thread around the spoke 3 times on the return.

Start again from the center, at A and work a ribbed backstitch wheel (see Lesson 23), wrapping the embroidery thread around the wrapped bars and the diagonal spokes. Go around the wheel 8 times.

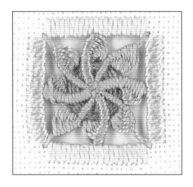

To form the petals, weave together each bar or diagonal spoke with the outside row of the wheel. Weave all the way up the bar or spoke to the satin stitches.

To move from one petal to the next, stop with the embroidery thread at the wheel and up against the next bar or spoke, then weave over or under that spoke as before to begin the next petal.

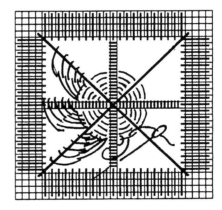

Some designs use smaller edelweiss filling stitches, like the ones shown below. In this case, make a smaller ribbed wheel, going around the wheel only about 5 times.

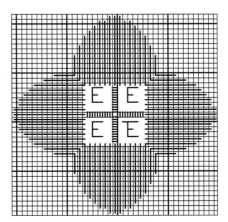

Lesson 28:
Shuttle Stitch

Instructions

Work the kloster blocks, then cut and remove the threads.

Use pearl cotton size 8 for 25 ct fabric or pearl cotton size 12 for 32 ct fabric.

Work the woven bars.

Then, work each open square separately.

The first step is to make a double arch. To do this, bring the embroidery thread from A to B, leaving enough slack that the thread forms a half-circle shape; return from B to A in the same way, inserting the needle on the bottom side of the work and coming out on the top side.

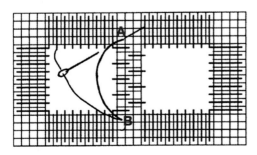

The second step is to work buttonhole stitches over the threads making the arch.

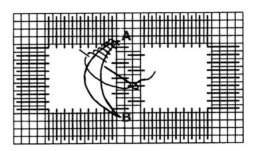

Do the same thing in the second open square, being careful to make the second arch the same size as the first one.

Here is a very pretty variation:

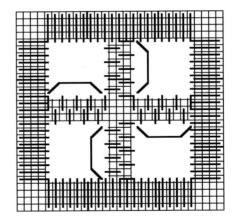

Lesson 29:
Buttonhole Arch Filling Stitch

Instructions

Work the kloster blocks, then cut and remove the threads.

Use pearl cotton size 8 for 25 ct fabric or pearl cotton size 12 for 32 ct fabric.

Make the woven bars.

The first step in making this filling stitch is to create a circle by adding a thread running from the center of each bar to the center of the next, returning in the opposite direction.

This is completed as follows:
• secure the embroidery thread at the center of one of the 4 woven bars,
• insert the needle through the back side of the bar and bring it up to the top side,
• bring the needle to the next bar and insert it again on the bottom side of the bar and bring it up to the top side,
• continue to work in the same manner until you're back at the starting point.

Then return in the same way, so that the threads cross each other.

The second step is to work buttonhole stitches back over this circle of thread, as for the shuttle stitch (Lesson 28).

When you reach the next bar, insert the needle from the top and bring it out on the bottom in the next arch of the circle.

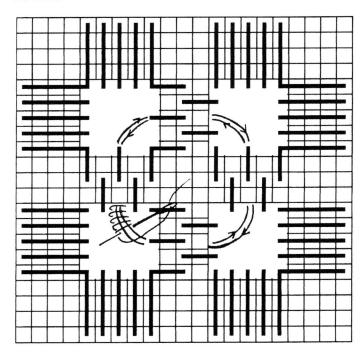

Lesson 30:
Buttonhole Stitch Circle

Instructions

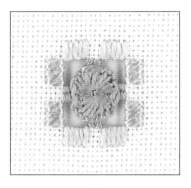

Work the kloster blocks, then cut and remove the threads.

Use pearl cotton size 8 for 25 ct fabric or pearl cotton size 12 for 32 ct fabric.

Make the 4 woven bars.

The first step in making this filling stitch is to create a double circle of thread about one-third of the way out from the center.

This is done as follows:
• secure the embroidery thread one-third of the way up one of the 4 woven bars,
• insert the needle from the back side of the bar and bring it out on the top side,
• carry the thread to the next bar, inserting the needle again from the back side and bringing it out on the top,
• continue to work in the same manner until you're back at the starting point.

Then go back around the circle in the same manner. This allows the threads to cross each other, making a firmer base for the buttonhole stitches.

The second step is to embroider over the circle just made using the buttonhole stitch, inserting the needle in the center of the motif and using the circle as support. There must always be the same number of stitches—in this case, 3—between each pair of woven bars.

In addition, make one buttonhole stitch in each bar, inserting the needle in the center of the bar.

The buttonhole circle made in this manner seems to float on the surface.

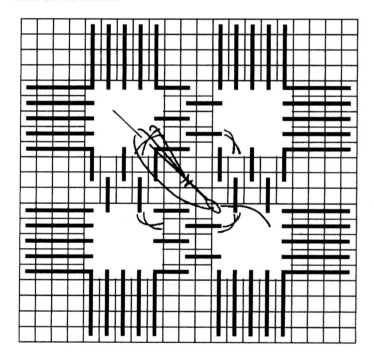

Lesson 31:
Buttonhole Stitch Flower

Instructions

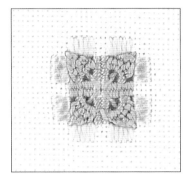

Work the kloster blocks, then cut and remove the threads.

Use pearl cotton size 8 for 25 ct fabric or pearl cotton size 12 for 32 ct fabric.

Make the woven bars.

Then make a twisted diagonal bar (see Lesson 15) from each corner to the middle, twisting the thread around the bar 2 times on the return.

The first step in making this filling stitch is to create a double circle of thread through the centers of the woven bars.

This is done as follows:
• bring the embroidery thread up at the middle of one of the 4 woven bars,
• bring the needle to the next bar, inserting it through the back side of the bar and bringing it out on the top,
• continue to work in the same manner until you're back at the starting point, then go back in the same manner.

Note: The circle must go over the twisted bars.

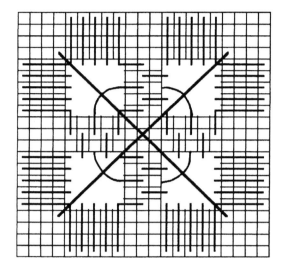

The second step is to work the 4 petals in buttonhole stitch. Each petal is worked separately.

Work as follows:
• Secure the embroidery thread under one of the woven bars and come out next to the circle on the front side of the work,
• using the circle as a base, work 7 buttonhole stitches from left to right, from one woven bar to the next,
• when you have stitched across one open square, work another row of buttonhole stitch in the first row in the opposite direction, starting by inserting the needle between the last two stitches of the previous row and ending bewteen the first two stitches, so that the second row has 5 buttonhole stitches,
• continue in this manner, with 3 buttonhole stitches in the third row and 1 in the last,
• to secure the embroidery thread, insert it in the starting stitch of the twisted bar.

Repeat these steps for each petal.

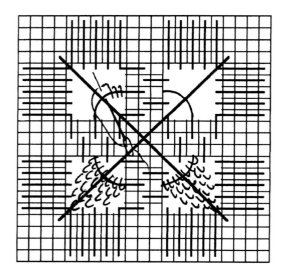

Lesson 32:
Woven Flower

Instructions

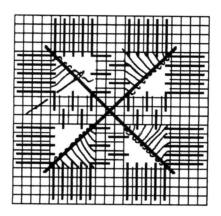

Work the kloster blocks, then cut and remove the threads.

Use pearl cotton size 8 for 25 ct fabric or pearl cotton size 12 for 32 ct fabric.

Work the woven bars.

Make a diagonl twisted bar (see Lesson 15) from each corner to the center, wrapping the thread around the bar twice on the return.

The flower is formed of 4 triangular petals. Each petal is worked in one half of an open square. Work each petal by using a diagonal twisted bar as the support on one side and a satin stitch block and woven bar on the other. To weave the petal, start on the outside edge and work towards the center, inserting the needle between each pair of satin stitches before the corner; after the corner, insert the needle in the center of the woven bar. At the same time, on the opposite side, bring the embroidery thread around the diagonal twisted bar.

Note: The weaving should be somewhat loose.

Lesson 33: Clover Filling Stitch

Instructions

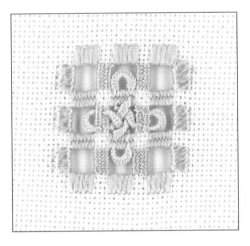

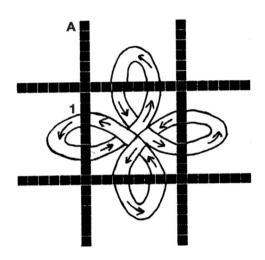

Work the kloster blocks, then cut and remove the threads.

For ease in stitching, use pearl cotton size 12 for 25 ct fabric.

Work as follows:
- start at point 1 in the diagram, two-thirds of the way up bar A,
- insert the needle in the bar from the back side, coming out on the top,
- insert the needle back into the same woven bar from the back, one-third of the way from the bottom, leaving a semicircle loop of thread,
- bring the needle out on top and return to point 1, twisting the thread once around the loop just made,
- insert the needle into the bar from the bottom, coming out on top,
- return, working buttonhole stitch over the loop.

Continue in the same manner, creating and embroidering loops in the order and directions indicated by the arrows, being sure to go over and under the other embroidered threads as indicated.

Lesson 34:
Drunkard's Path

Instructions

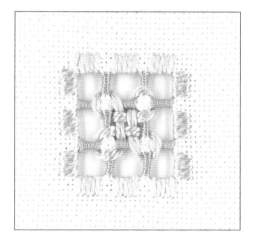

Work the kloster blocks, then cut and remove the threads.

Use pearl cotton size 8 for 25 ct fabric or pearl cotton size 12 for 32 ct fabric.

Work the wrapped bars over 4 fabric threads.

Switch to pearl cotton size 5 for 25 ct fabric or pearl cotton size 8 for 32 ct fabric and position the embroidery thread at the intersection of the 4 bars at the top left corner (A).

Then follow the path indicated by the arrows, passing the thread over and under the bars and the other embroidery threads as indicated in the diagram.

Take the embroidery thread through this same path a second time.

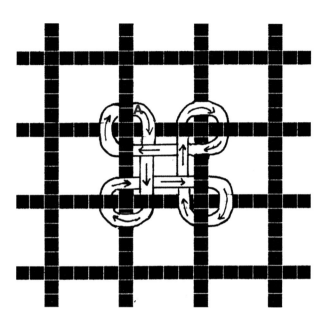

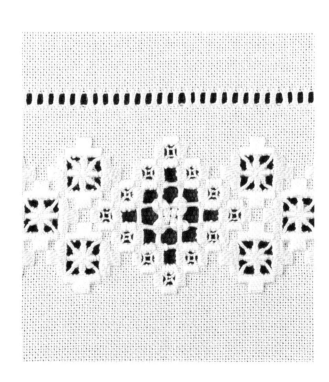

Lesson 35: Leaf

Instructions

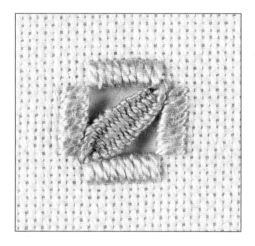

Work kloster blocks, then cut and remove the threads. Work any surrounding woven bars indicated in the design.

Use pearl cotton size 8 for 25 ct fabric or pearl cotton size 12 for 32 ct fabric.

Make 2 taut diagonal stitches from 1 to 2, then from 2 back to 1. These threads will act as the inside framework of the leaf.

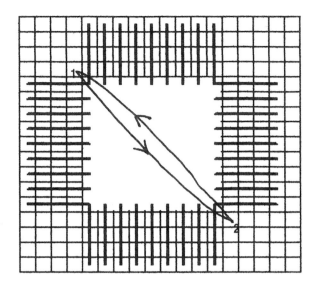

Form the final base for the leaf by placing a looser thread on each side of the first ones, make 4 diagonal threads.

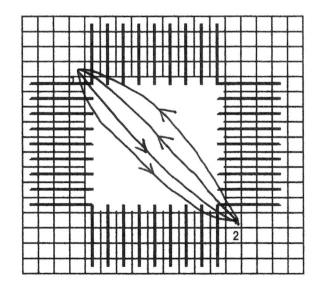

Now it's time to make the leaf. To do this, weave between the center spoke comprised of 2 threads (AB) and the two outside looser threads (C and D).

Weave the embroidery thread:
• over C,
• under AB,
• over D.

Turn the needle and continue weaving by bringing the embroidery thread:
• under D,
• over AB,
• under C.

Turn the needle and continue weaving in the same manner.

While weaving, keep the diagonal threads between the thumb and index finger of your free hand, making sure there is enough space between threads AB in the center and C and D on the outside. There should be very little space at the beginning and end of the leaf and more space in the middle in order for it to take on the shape of a leaf.

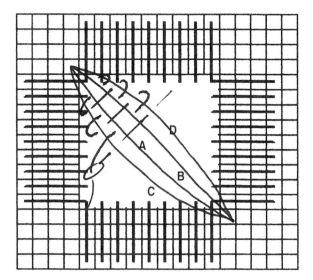

Lesson 36: Flower Filling Stitch

Instructions

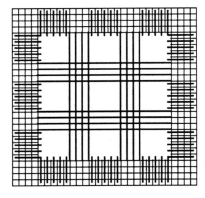

Work the kloster blocks, then cut and remove the threads.

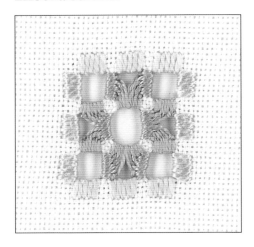

Use pearl cotton size 8 for 25 ct fabric or pearl cotton size 12 for 32 ct fabric.

Work wrapped bar 1 over 4 fabric threads.

Then embroider between bar 1 and half of bar 2, in the following manner:
• position the needle at A, (the last wrap around bar 1 should go over the bar and then down into the square with A as a corner),

• then move the needle to B, passing under bars 1 and 2, pulling the embroidery thread,
• return to A, with the embroidery thread passing over bar 2, then over bar 1,
• wrap the thread around bar 1, coming up in the corner between the two bars, and inserting the needle to the left of the embroidery thread from the previous step; pull,
• pass over the last embroidery thread, then under bar 2 to return to B, and start the steps over again with the third step.

Continue in this way until bar 2 is covered halfway.

Work the other corners in the same manner, forming a circle.

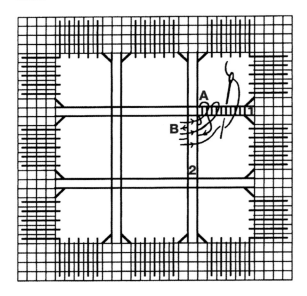

Lesson 37:
Drawn Thread Work Beginning and Ending near the Edge

This technique is used for hemstitching inside a motif or to prepare mitered corners with drawn threadwork.

Instructions

Cut the number of threads shown in the pattern (usually 4), starting from the center of the drawn thread area in order to leave enough thread length to be able to weave the threads back in.

Pull the threads out carefully up to each corner and slip them to the back side of the work.

With a needle, insert the threads back through the weave of the fabric, going over and under about 4 times.

To secure these threads, work a buttonhole stitch over 2 to 4 fabric threads, or even a satin stitch kloster block over 4 fabric threads when the embroidery stitch allows.

Cut the drawn threads short.

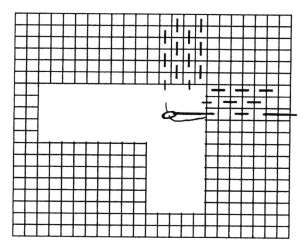

Lesson 38: Mitered Corners

Mitered corners are used when the hem measures at least 1 inch.

Instructions

First decide the width of the final hem, 1¼ in. (3 cm) for example. Then plan for a margin between the motif and the place where the hem will be sewn or embroidered with mitered corners. When the pattern includes hemstitching around the perimeter, use that as a baseline.

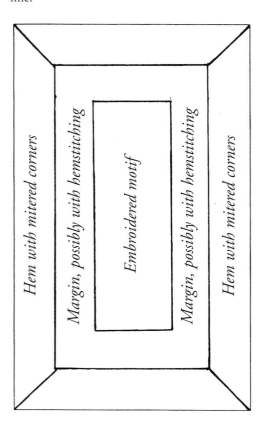

Take the following steps to prepare mitered corners:
- count 30 fabric threads (about 1¼ in. or 3 cm for 25 ct fabric) starting from the baseline selected or from the drawn thread work, then sew basting line A,
- count another 30 fabric threads and sew basting line B,
- finally, count 10 fabric threads, remove the next thread (C), and cut cleanly following the drawn thread opening obtained,
- work overcast stitch.

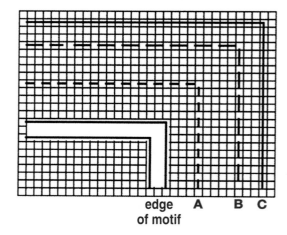

edge of motif   A   B   C

Press with an iron to help shape the corners throughout the following folding steps.

Fold the fabric in at the four corners to bring corner D and basting line B together.

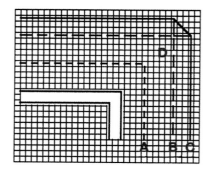

Fold fabric over so that edge C meets basting line B. The corners should touch, but not overlap.

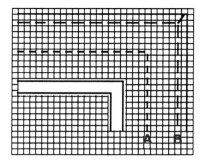

Fold the corners in again as in the first step: corner E meets basting line A.

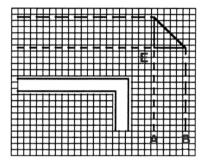

Fold the sides in again as in the second step, so that edge B meets basting line A.

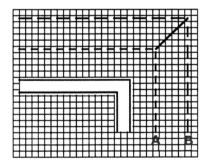

The corners now have their final shape. However, to avoid excessive thickness, the extra fabric must be cut.

To do this, reopen the folds and draw a pencil line G about ½ inch (1 cm) from the outside edge of fold F.

Cut along this line to trim off the blacked-out area in the diagram below.

Work overcast stitch along edge G.

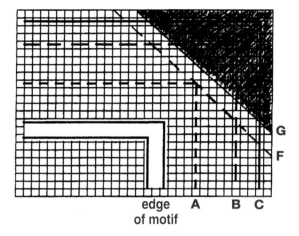

Refold the fabric and baste through all the layers in order to hold the work together.

Sew or embroider a regular hemstitch, ladder hemstitch, zigzag hemstitch, or other hemstitch along the edge.

Lesson 39:
Ladder Hemstitch

This stitch works equally as well as a border or as a decorative stitch inside a motif.

Instructions

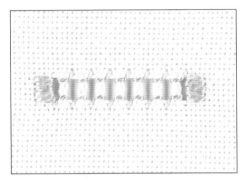

Use pearl cotton size 8 for 25 ct fabric or pearl cotton size 12 for 32 ct fabric.

Work on the back side of the fabric, from left to right for right-handers and from right to left for left-handers.

Cut and remove threads as indicated on your pattern, prepare the edge and the corners, and baste. Refer to Lessons 37 and 38 for best methods.

Work the hemstitch as follows:
- bring up the embroidery thread at the edge at point B, through all the thicknesses of fabric if you are working an embroidered hem,
- count down the next 4 warp fabric threads and insert the needle between the fourth and the 5th thread, at point A.
- bring the needle back out on the back of the work at point C, 2 fabric threads above B.

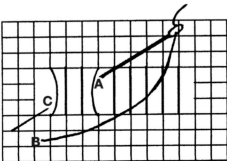

Continue in this manner:
- insert the needle again at point A on the right side,
- then, come out again on the back side at point D, 2 weft fabric threads below the drawn thread area and at 4 warp fabric threads from point B.

Start again at the beginning of the steps.

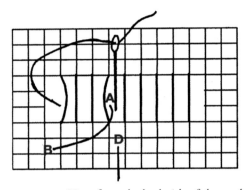

View from the back side of the work.

To complete the ladder hemstitch, start the steps again on the opposite side of the drawn threads, again on the back side of the work.

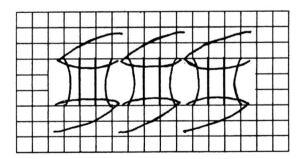

Lesson 40:
Zigzag Hemstitch

This stitch works equally as well as a border or as a decorative stitch inside a motif.

Instructions

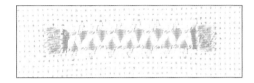

Use pearl cotton size 8 for 25 ct fabric or size 12 for 32 ct fabric.

Work on the wrong side of the fabric, from left to right for right-handers and from right to left for left-handers.

Cut and remove threads as indicated on your pattern, prepare the edge and the corners; baste. Refer to Lessons 37 and 38 for best methods.

Work as follows:
- bring up the embroidery thread at the edge at point B, through all thicknesses of fabric if you are working an embroidered hem,
- count down the next 4 warp fabric threads and insert the needle between the fourth and the fifth threads, at point A.

The embroidery thread passes over the right side of the work, circles around the 4 warp fabric threads and returns to the back side at point C, 2 fabric threads above B.

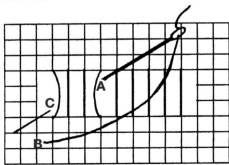

View from the back side of the work.

Continue in this manner:
- take the needle back to the right side, inserting it again at point A,
- then come up again on the back side at point D, 2 weft fabric threads below the drawn thread area and 4 warp fabric threads from point B.

Start again at the beginning of the steps.

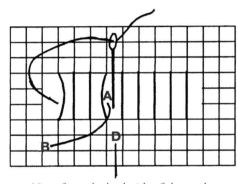

View from the back side of the work.

To make the zigzag hemstitch, start the steps again, still working on the back side, but on the opposite side of the drawn threads, with the stitches staggered, meaning the stitches are worked starting two threads down from those on the first side.

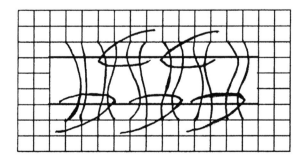

Lesson 41:
Venetian Wrapped Hemstitch

This stitch works equally as well as a border or as a decorative stitch inside a motif.

Instructions

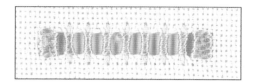

Use pearl cotton size 8 for 25 ct fabric or pearl cotton size 12 for 32 ct fabric.

Cut and remove threads as indicated on your pattern. Prepare the edge and the corners and baste. Refer to Lessons 37 and 38 for best methods.

Work on the right side of the fabric. With embroidery thread make wrapped bars over 4 fabric threads, working as follows:

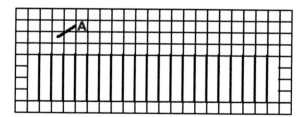

Bring the needle up 2 fabric threads above the drawn thread area and in the middle of the first 4 fabric threads, at A.

Bring the thread down across the drawn thread area and insert the needle 2 threads below it. This additional thread will give more strength to the bar.

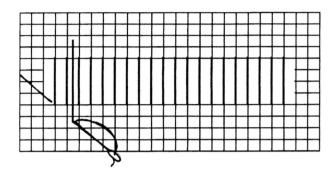

Wrap the embroidery thread around these 5 threads, working up the bar.

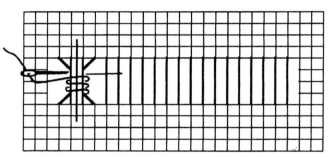

Finish the bar by inserting the needle through the back side of the fabric 4 fabric threads to the side and 2 threads above the drawn threads, in the middle of the next 4 fabric threads.

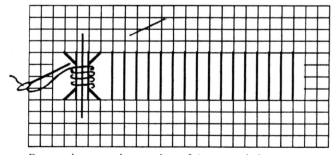

Repeat the steps the number of times needed.

Lesson 42:
Double Zigzag Hemstitch

This stitch works equally as well as a border or as a decorative stitch inside a motif.

Instructions

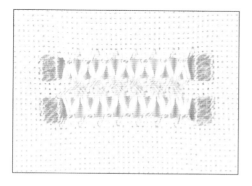

Use pearl cotton size 8 for 25 ct fabric or pearl cotton size 12 for 32 ct fabric.

Cut and draw threads as shown in the design, 2 or 3 times, or more as needed. Prepare the edge, miter the corners, and baste. Refer to Lessons 37 and 38 for best methods.

Then, work as follows:
• First complete the zigzag hemstitch along the two outermost edges of the drawn thread area (see Lesson 40).

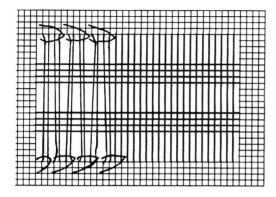

• Next, work a herringbone stitch on the right side of the fabric.

Follow the numbers in the diagram to complete this stitch.

The dotted lines indicate where the embroidery thread passes under the fabric, and the solid lines show where it is on the top side.

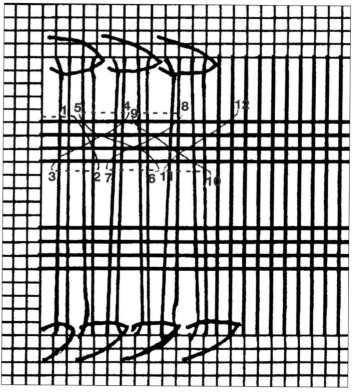

This stitch can be embroidered over 2 rows of drawn threadwork instead of 3.

Lesson 43:
Interlaced Hemstitch

This stitch works equally as well as a border or as a decorative stitch inside a motif.
The ladder hemstitch may be worked over 2 or 4 threads instead of using the four-sided stitch.

Instructions

A – Interlaced Hemstitch with Embroidery Thread

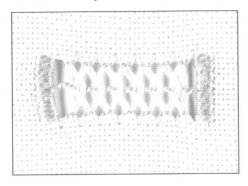

Work satin stitches with pearl cotton size 5, then the four-sided stitch with pearl cotton size 5 or size 8, for 25 ct fabric, depending on the effect desired (for 32 ct fabric, use pearl cotton size 8 or size 12).

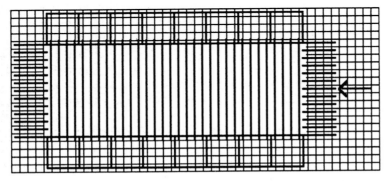

Cut and remove all the horizontal threads, leaving the vertical ones.

Work from right to left on the right side:
• come up at A,
• insert the needle at B, then come up at C,
• bring the 2 fabric threads on the left over the 2 fabric threads on the right,
• insert the needle at D, then flip it over so it points back to the left, twisting the 2 bundles of thread.

Pull tight. The embroidery thread will go between the crossed threads and hold them in place.

Begin the steps again with the next 4 threads.

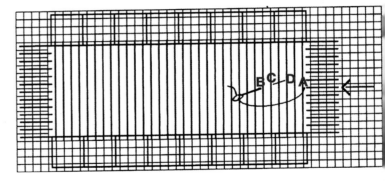

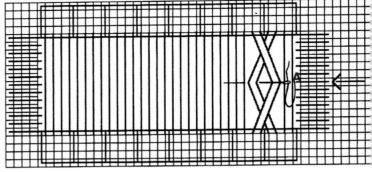

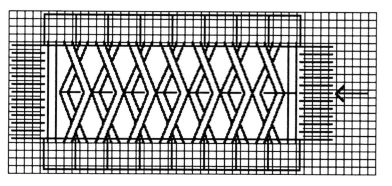

B – Interlaced Hemstitch with Ribbon

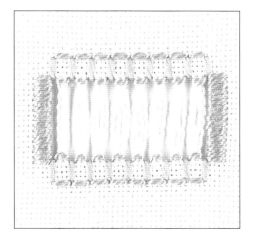

Work in the same manner as in section A, but use a 1/8 in. (3 mm) satin ribbon instead of embroidery thread.

In addition, it will work better if you make the drawn thread area a little taller—17 satin stitches tall instead of 13.

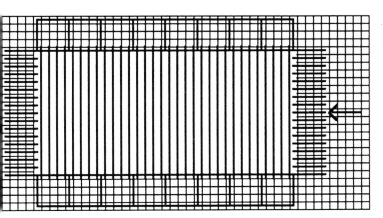

C – Interlaced Crossed Ladder Hemstitch over 2 Rows

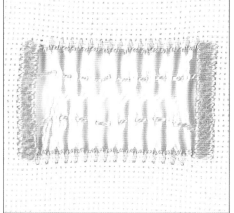

Work the satin stitches, then cut and remove all the horizontal fabric threads, leaving the vertical ones.

Work the ladder hemstitch over 2 fabric threads on the top and bottom edges.

Then work the interlaced stitch as in example A, but 2 times: once where indicated by the top arrow, and a second time at the level of the lower arrow, staggering the rows.

Mini Cushions

Materials

Small amounts of 25 ct Lugana fabric, any color
Pearl cotton size 5, any color
Size 22 tapestry needle
Embroidery hoop
Fiberfill or other stuffing
Ribbon or cord
Small amounts of quilting fabric for lining

Stitch used

Satin Stitch (Lesson 1)

*The size of the finished cushions will depend on the motifs selected. On average, they will be squares of about 2–3"
(5–7 cm).*

Instructions

The best way to proceed is to embroider several motifs one after the other on evenweave fabric remnants and then cut the pieces out to the right size. This will allow you to work on pieces large enought to use an embroidery hoop with.

Always begin in the center of your motif.

Once your motifs are finished, simply stuff your little cushions with fiberfill and sew them up, inserting a ribbon or cord in the middle of one side or at a corner, depending on the look desired.

Diagrams

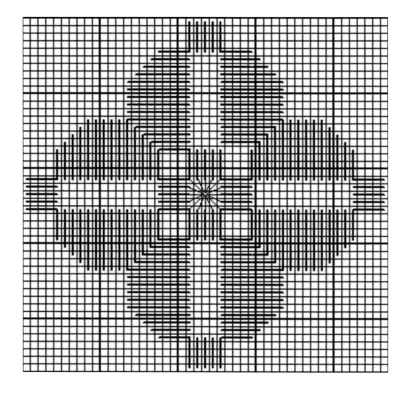

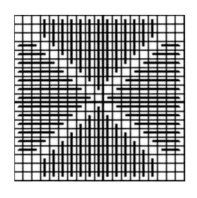

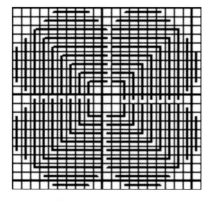

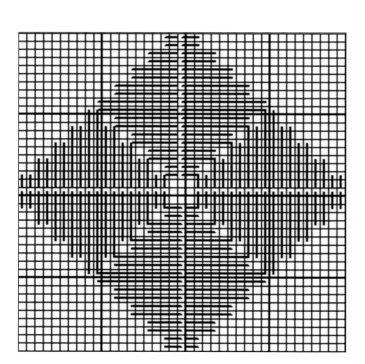

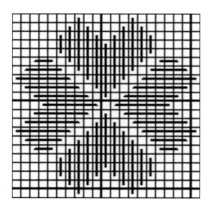

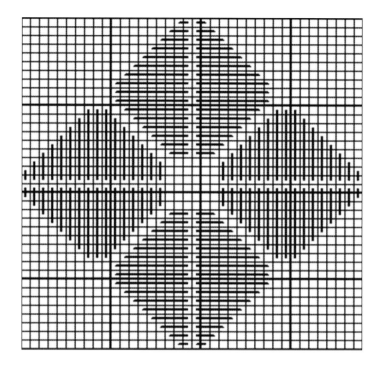

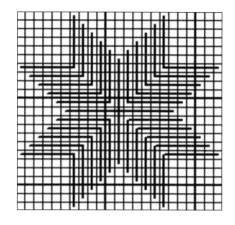

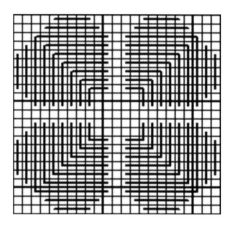

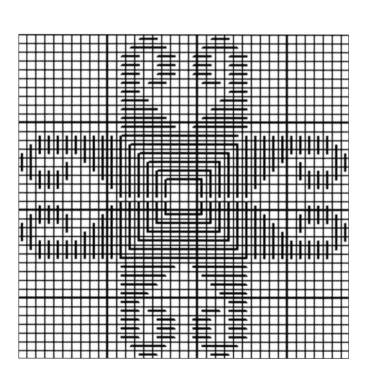

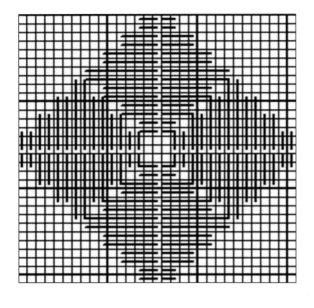

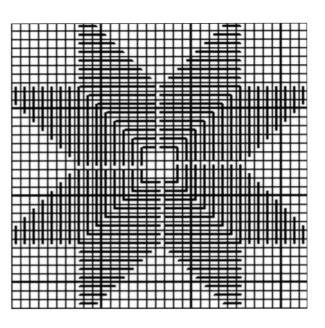

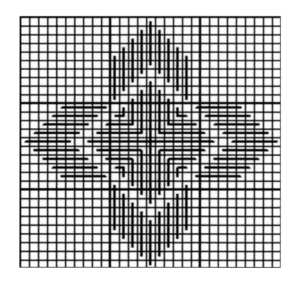

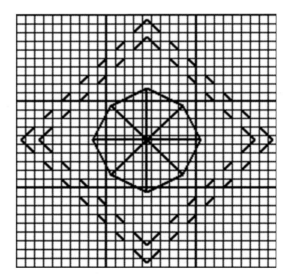

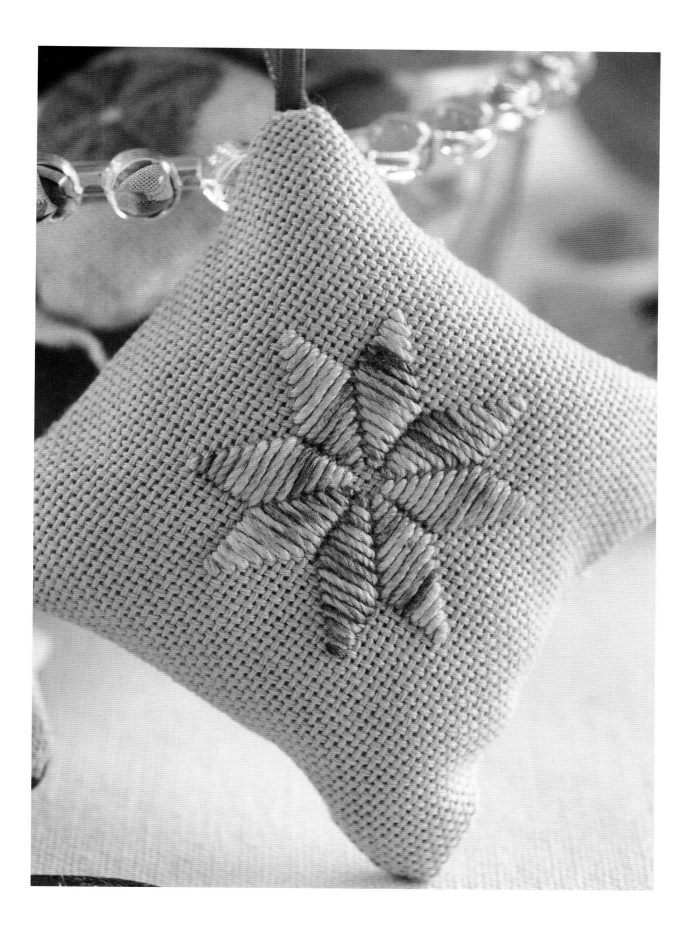

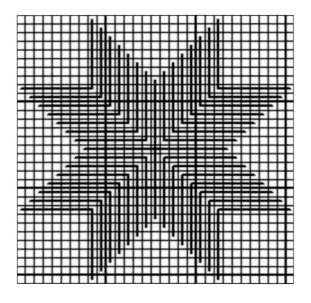

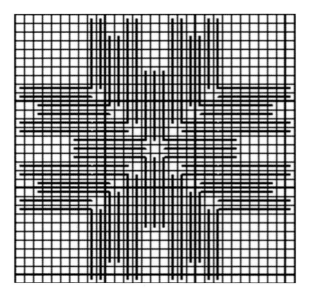

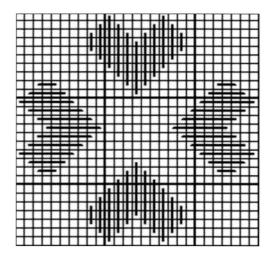

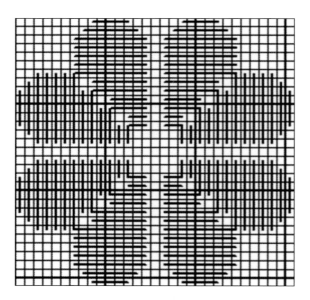

Berlingot Baubles

Materials

For bauble 1—3¹/₂" x 5" (9 x 13 cm)
25 ct Lugana Fein-Floba fabric, 3¹/₂" x 5" (9 x 13 cm), color no. 53 (Oatmeal)
DMC Pearl cotton sizes 5 and 8, color no. 223
Size 22 and 24 tapestry needles
Embroidery hoop
8" (20 cm) of ribbon or cord
Quilting fabric for lining: 3¹/₂" x 5" (9 x 13 cm)
1 tassel
Fiberfill

For bauble 2—3¹/₂" x 6" (9 x 15 cm)
32 ct Murano fabric, 3¹/₂" x 6" (9 x 15 cm), color no. 264 (Ivory)
DMC pearl cotton sizes 8 and 12, color no. 842
Sizes 24 and 26 tapestry needles
Embroidery hoop
8" (20 cm) of ribbon or cord
Quilting fabric for the lining: 3¹/₂" x 6" (9 x 15 cm)
1 tassel
Fiberfill

Stitches used

For bauble 1
Satin Stitch (Lesson 1)
Woven Bars (Lesson 4)
Madeira Star (Lesson 6C)

For bauble 2
Satin Stitch (Lesson 1)
Woven Bars (Lesson 4)
Dove's Eye Filling Stitch (Lesson 7)
Picots (Lesson 8)

Instructions

These little pouches are great for small, personalized gifts. They can be used as key rings or scented sachets, be attached to a cabinet or drawer knob, or be hung as Christmas tree ornaments. A larger one can be used as a mini-purse (see page 80). This project is a good place to try novelty embroidery threads.

Bauble 1
Find the center of the fabric by folding it in half one way and then the other. Count 14 threads from the center to the top of the first kloster block and embroider first the small diamond shape, then the large one.

Cut and remove the threads, then work the woven bars.

Finish by working the center star in satin stitch, and then the Madeira stars.

Bauble 2
Find the center of the fabric by folding it in half one way and then the other. Count 34 threads from the center to the outside edge of the kloster blocks on the right and work the outline of blocks around the rectangle, then complete the diagonal sides of the two corner triangles.

Cut and remove the threads. Work the woven bars, the dove's eye filling stitches, and the picots at the same time.

Assembly

To make the tassel, cut a piece of cardboard 2" (5 cm) wide. Wind the pearl cotton around the 2" (5 cm) length about 30 times. At one end, slip 2 threads between the cardboard and the wound pearl cotton, and tie together tightly. Cut the opposite end of the loops. Wind another piece of pearl cotton around the threads several times to form the head of the tassel.

To assemble the bauble, line it, then fold it in half (the fold line is indicated by dotted lines), right side to right side, and sew together the two sides AC and BD. Slip in the tassel at the fold of side AC.

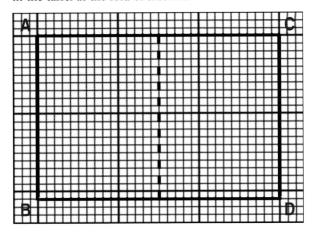

Turn right side out and whipstitch together the remaining side, with the seams (AC and BD) meeting in the center of the new seam. Position the cord at one end of this seam.

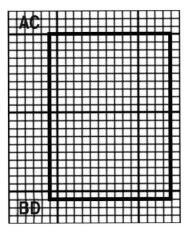

Key 1

Kloster Blocks

Woven Bars

Madeira Star

Diagram 1

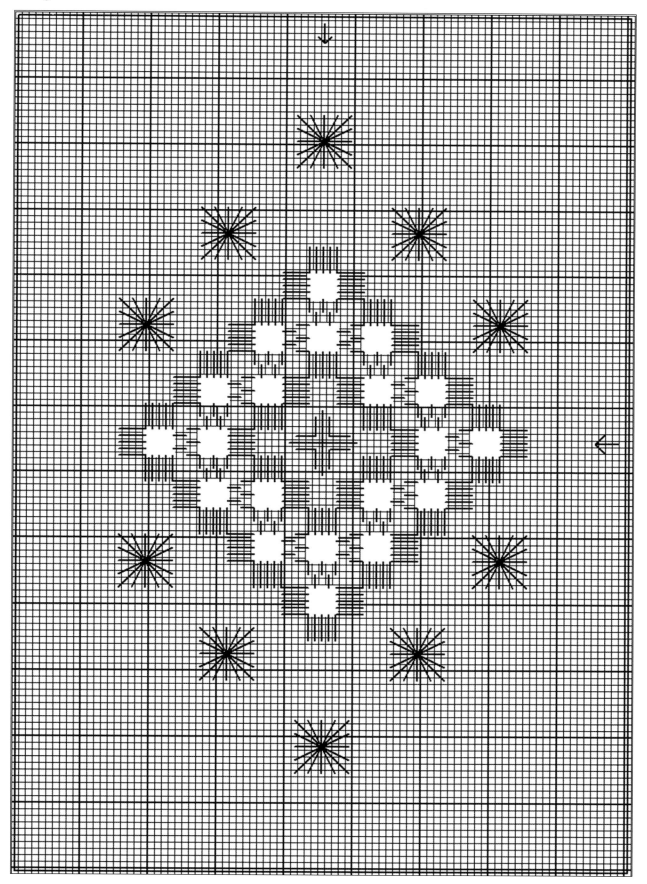

Diagram 2

Key 2

Kloster Blocks

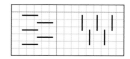

Woven Bars

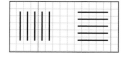

Dove's Eye Filling Stitch

Picots

Berlingot Pouch

Materials

32 ct Murano fabric, 10" x 17" (25 x 43 cm), color no. 264 (Ivory)
DMC pearl cotton sizes 8 and 12, color no. 842
Sizes 24 and 26 tapestry needles
Embroidery hoop
12" (30 cm) of ⅛" (3 mm) satin ribbon for interlaced hemstitch
8" (20 cm) of matching ribbon for the strap
Two pieces of quilting fabric in different colors for the lining: 8" x 15" (20 x 38 cm) (one for inside the pouch, the other to line the drawn threadwork)
7" (18 cm) zipper

Stitches used

Satin Stitch (Lesson 1)
Interlaced Hemstitch with Ribbon (Lesson 43B)
Interlaced Crossed Ladder Hemstitch over 2 Rows (Lesson 43C)
Double Zigzag Hemstitch (Lesson 42)
Zigzag Hemstitch (Lesson 40)
Ladder Hemstitch (Lesson 39)
Diagonal Triple Cable Stitch (Lesson 13E)
Four-Sided Stitch (Lesson 10)

The berlingot pouch measures 8" x 15" (20 x 38 cm).

Instructions

Begin by working the border in satin stitch and Scandinavian four-sided stitch using pearl cotton size 8, working the two stitches simultaneously, which will help keep a correct count of stitches. The border will have 49 four-sided stitches on the short sides, and 108 on the long sides.

Then work the hemstitch interlaced with ribbon in the center of the piece, beginning with the ladder hemstitch on each side (using pearl cotton size 12 for the ladder hemstitch).

Then, following the diagram, work the various stitches in mirror image on either side of the central pulled threadwork:
• the satin stitch motifs with pearl cotton size 8,
• the triple zigzag hemstitch (first complete the zigzag hemstitch on both sides, using pearl cotton size 12),
• diagonal triple cable stitch with pearl cotton size 12,
• and finally, the interlaced crossed ladder hemstitch, using pearl cotton size 8 to make it stand out more. Be sure to work the ladder hemstitch on each side first using pearl cotton size 12.

Pull a thread around the edge, about ¾" (2 cm), or 24 fabric threads, from the outside edge of the satin stitch border. This will give you an 8" x 15" (20 x 38 cm) rectangle.

Line the embroidered piece with the selected fabric and zigzag stitch around the edge.

To insert the zipper (it is important that the zipper be placed on the shorter side of the rectangle, meaning the 8 in. side, at A—see diagram 1):
• At A, place the wrong side of the zipper edge to edge on the right side of the lining fabric.
• Pin.

- Next, place the right side of the embroidery against the right side of the zipper. Pin. Sew together 3/8" (8 mm) from the edge, turn over, and topstitch 1/16" (1 mm) from the zippper.

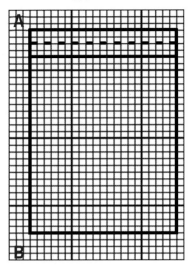

Zipper

Assemble side B in the same manner. To topstitch along this seam (optional), open the zipper. At this point you will have a tube with the zipper in the middle.

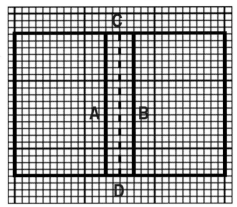

Make a seam on the wrong side of the work along side D, about 1/2" (1 cm) from the edge, with the bottom of the zipper in the middle of the seam. Topstitch.

On side C, fold the pouch in half the opposite way from seam D, so the beginning of the zipper is at one end of the seam. Remember to sew the small loop of ribbon that will act as a little strap into this seam. Stitch on the reverse side, then topstitch.

Turn right side out, and your pouch is finished!

Key

Kloster Blocks

Ladder Hemstitch for Interlaced Hemstitch

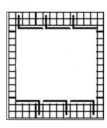

Zigzag Hemstitch for Triple Zigzag Hemstitch

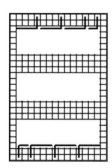

Variations on the Cable Stitch

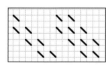

Scandinavian Four-Sided Stitch

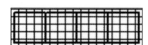

Diagram

This diagram shows half of the piece. The other half is its mirror image.

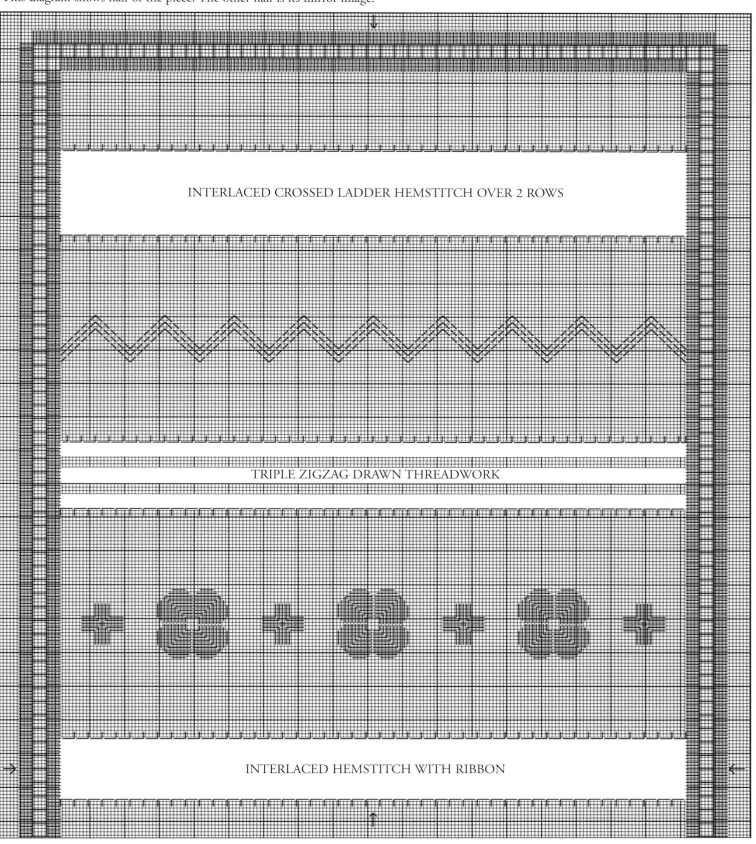

INTERLACED CROSSED LADDER HEMSTITCH OVER 2 ROWS

TRIPLE ZIGZAG DRAWN THREADWORK

INTERLACED HEMSTITCH WITH RIBBON

Scissors Case

Materials

36 ct Edinburgh linen, 6" x 6" (15 x 15 cm), color no. 52 (Flax)

DMC Pearl cotton size 12, color no. 356

Size 26 tapestry needle

Embroidery hoop

20" (50 cm) of ⅛" (3 cm) wide sheer organza ribbon

Two pieces of quilting fabric for the lining: 6" x 6" (15 x 15 cm)

Stitches used

Ladder Hemstitch (Lesson 39)

Interlaced Hemstitch (Lesson 43)

Ribbed Wheel (Lesson 23)

The finished work measures 6" x 6" (15 x 15 cm).

Instructions

Cut a piece of fabric 6" x 6" (15 x 15 cm), beginning by pulling out a fabric thread so you cut with the grain. Overcast stitch around the edge.

At 25 fabric threads from the edge (about ¾" or 1.8 cm), remove 12 fabric threads (about ⅓" or 0.85 cm) from one end of the fabric to the other, on all 4 sides.

Work the ladder hemstitch over 4 fabric threads around the edges of the drawn thread area, then complete the interlaced hemstitch, and finish with the 4 ribbed wheels.

Now all you have left to do is assemble your case.

Zigzag stitch your embroidery to one of the lining fabrics, with the right side of the fabric against the wrong side of the embroidery. This makes a 6" x 6" (15 x 15 cm) lined square.

Place point B on point D, right sides together (see diagram on page 86). Make a seam ¼" (5 mm) from the edge from corner BD to C. Open the seam, turn the piece right side out, and bring the seam to the middle—from C to E.

Do exactly the same thing with the lining fabric, but without turning it right side out; the wrong side should still be out.

Then sew the lining and the embroidery together, right sides together, from A to D. Turn and tuck the lining inside the case (it is still wrong side out, so the inside will look nice). Finally, slipstitch from A to B.

Cut the ribbon in 2 pieces and sew one piece to the front of the case and the other to the tip of the flap.

Assembly

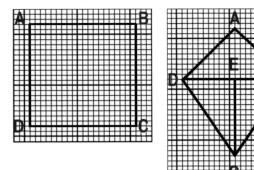 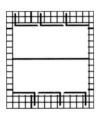

Key

Ladder Hemstitch and
Interlaced Hemstitch

Ribbed Wheel

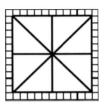

Diagram

The arrows and the cross indicate the center. Work the other three quarters of the piece in the same way.

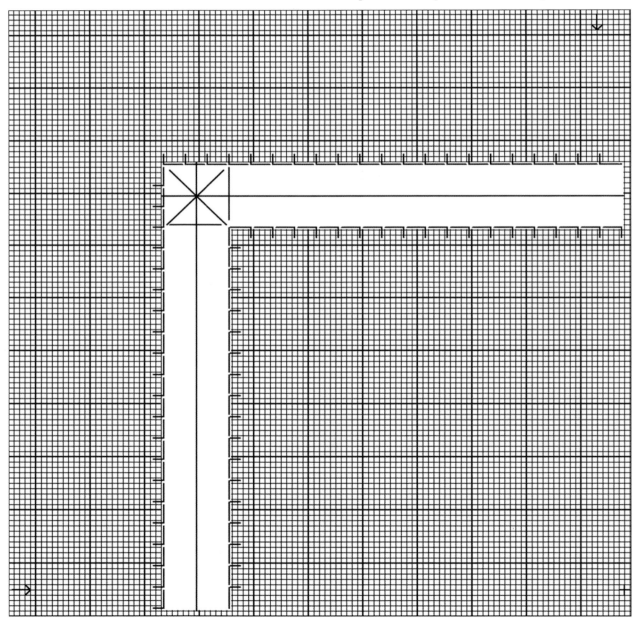

Star Motif Needle Case

Materials

25 ct Lugana fabric, color no. 501 (Wedgewood), 10" x 6" (25 x 15 cm) for the case cover and 6" x 4" (15 x 10 cm) for the case insert

DMC pearl cotton sizes 5 and 8, white

Size 22 and 24 tapestry needles

Embroidery hoop

Stitches used

Satin Stitch (Lesson 1)

Norwegian Star (Lesson 1B)

Eyelet Stitch (Lesson 6B)

Buttonhole Stitch (Lesson 9)

Variations on the Cable Stitch (Lesson 13)

When finished, the case cover will measure 7¼" x 3" (18.5 x 7.5) cm and the case insert 4⅛" x 2⅛" (10.5 x 5.5 cm).

Instructions

Case insert

Fold the fabric in half one way and then the other to find the middle.

Count 28 fabric threads from the center and work the buttonhole stitches.

When the border is finished, cut close to the edge.

Set aside until later.

Case cover

Fold the fabric in half one way and then the other to find the middle.

Begin by working the kloster blocks in one of the diamonds, starting 26 fabric threads from the center. Then work the second diamond.

Next work the buttonhole stitches around the edge, the eyelet stitches, and then the Norwegian stars.

Cut off the excess fabric around the buttonhole stitches.

Assembly

Iron both parts, being sure to mark the center fold of each.

Baste the two parts together, making sure the center folds are right on top of each other.

Stitch them together vertically using the double cable stitch down the middle. Work the diagonal double cable stitch on each side of the fold on the cover.

Key

Kloster Blocks

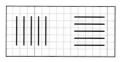

Norwegian Star

Eyelet Stitch

Buttonhole Stitch

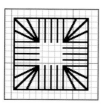

Variations on the Cable Stitch

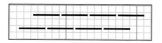

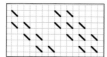

Diagrams

Case cover. The arrows indicate the center of the design.

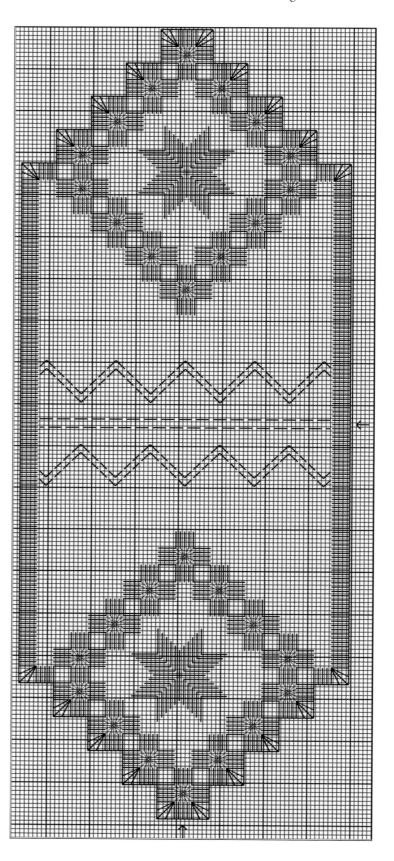

Close-up of motif

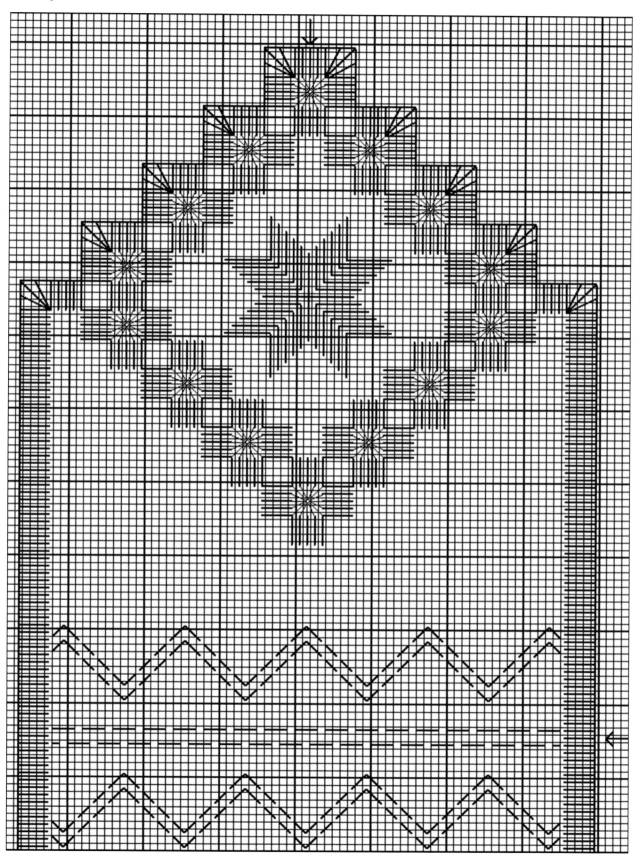

Case insert. The arrows indicate the center of the design.

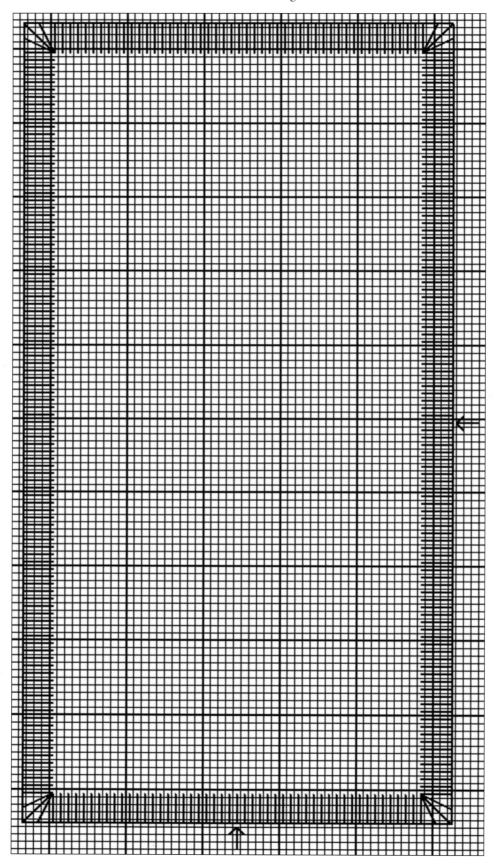

Flower Motif Needle Case

Materials
25 ct Lugana fabric, color no. 7729 (Vintage Grey), 10¼" x 6¼" (26 x 16 cm) for the outside case and 8¾" x 5½" (22 x 14 cm) for the inside case
DMC pearl cotton sizes 5 and 8, color white
Size 22 and 24 tapestry needles
Embroidery hoop

Stitches used
Satin Stitch (Lesson 1)
Variations on the Cable Stitch (Lesson 13)
Scandinavian Four-Sided Stitch (Lesson 10)

When finished, the case cover will measure 8" x 4" (20 x 10 cm) and the case insert 6¼" x 3⅛" (16 x 8 cm).

Instructions
Case insert
Fold the fabric in half one way and then the other to find the middle.

Count 40 fabric threads from the center and begin the first part of the Scandinavian four-sided stitch. When you have gone all the way around the edge, work the second side of the stitch.

When the border is finished, cut off the excess fabric from the back, close to the edge.

Set aside until later.

Case cover
Fold the fabric in half one way and then the other to find the middle.

Begin by working one of the kloster diamonds, starting 19 fabric threads from the center. Then work the second diamond on the opposite side.

Next work the satin stitch flower and the two diamond-shaped rows of cable stitch.

Finally, work the Scandinavian four-sided stitch around the edge, then cut off the extra fabric from the back side.

Assembly
Iron both parts, being sure to mark the center fold of each.

Baste the two parts together, making sure the center folds are right on top of each other.

Stitch them together vertically using the double cable stitch down the middle.

Key

Kloster Blocks

Variations on the Cable Stitch

Scandinavian Four-Sided Stitch

Diagrams

Case cover. The arrows indicate the center of the piece.

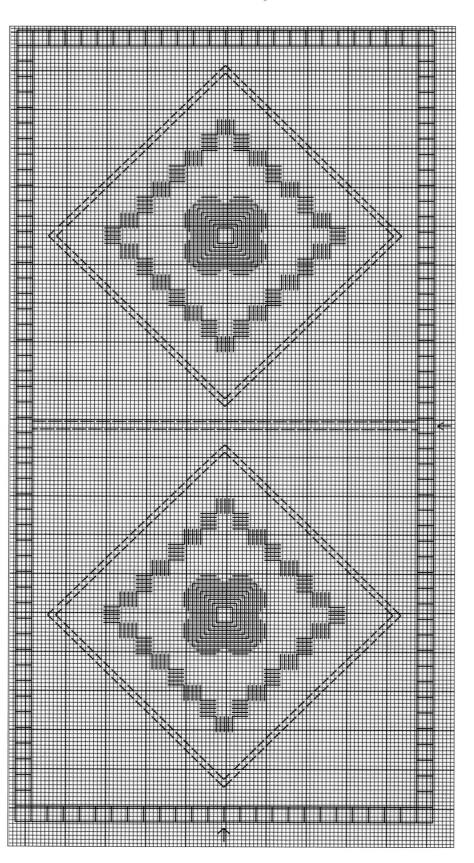

Case insert. The arrows indicate the center of the piece.

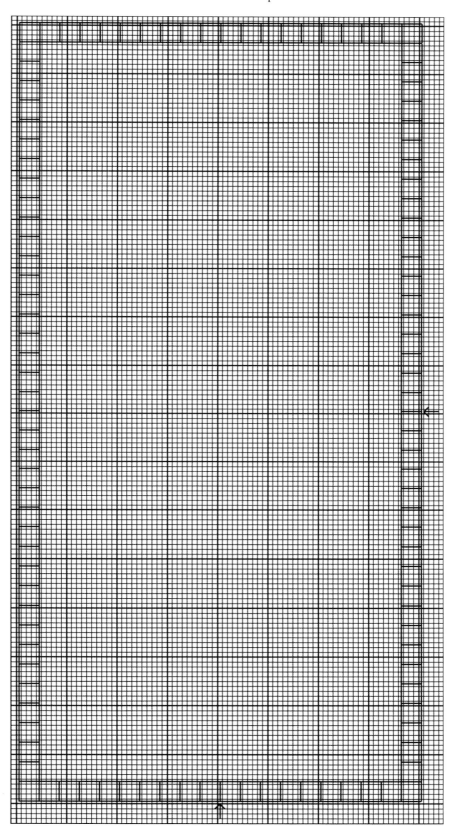

Scissors Keeper

Materials
25 ct Lugana fabric, 4¾" x 4¾" (12 x 12 cm), color
  no. 264 (Ivory)
DMC pearl cotton sizes 5 and 8, color no. 712
Size 22 and 24 tapestry needles
Embroidery hoop
Two pieces of quilting fabric 3¼" x 3¼" (8.5 x 8.5 cm)
  per cushion
Fiberfill
1 tassel per scissors keeper
12" length of matching cord for each scissors keeper

Stitches used
Satin Stitch (Lesson 1)
Woven Bars (Lesson 4)
Eyelet Stitch (Lesson 6B)
Dove's Eye Filling Stitch (Lesson 7)

*The finished motifs measure 3" x 3" (7.5 x 7.5 cm) and
the assembled scissors keepers are 3¼" x 3¼" (8.5 x 8.5
cm).*

Instructions

Design 1

Find the middle of the fabric by folding it in half one way and then the other.

Count up 30 fabric threads towards the top and begin stitching the kloster blocks that form the inside diamond. Then work the outside diamond and the square.

Cut and remove the threads in every other small square. Work the dove's eye filling stitch in the open squares and the eyelet stitch in the others.

Finally, cut and remove the threads in the center diamond. Work the woven bars and dove's eye filling stitches at the same time.

Line the embroidery using a zigzag stitch to attach one of the lining fabrics (right side of lining to wrong side of embroidery).

Sew the the lined piece of embroidery and the remaining piece of lining fabric together into a pillow and stuff with fiberfill, attaching a small cord in one corner and a tassel in the opposite corner.

Design 2

Find the middle of the fabric by folding it in half one way and then the other.

Count up 30 fabric threads towards the top and begin stitching the kloster blocks forming the inside diamond. Then work the outside diamond and the square.

Cut and remove the threads in every other small square. Work the dove's eye filling stitch in the open squares and the eyelet stitch in the others.

Cut and remove the threads in the 4 corners of the square and work the woven bars.

Finally, cut and remove the threads in the center diamond. Work the woven bars and dove's eye filling stitches at the same time.

Line the embroidery using a zigzag stitch to attach one of the lining fabrics (right side of lining to wrong side of embroidery).

Assemble the lined embroidery and the remaining piece of lining fabric together into a pillow and stuff with the fiberfill, attaching a small cord in one corner and a tassel in the opposite corner.

Key

Kloster Blocks	Woven Bars	Dove's Eye Filling Stitch	Eyelet Stitch

Diagram 1

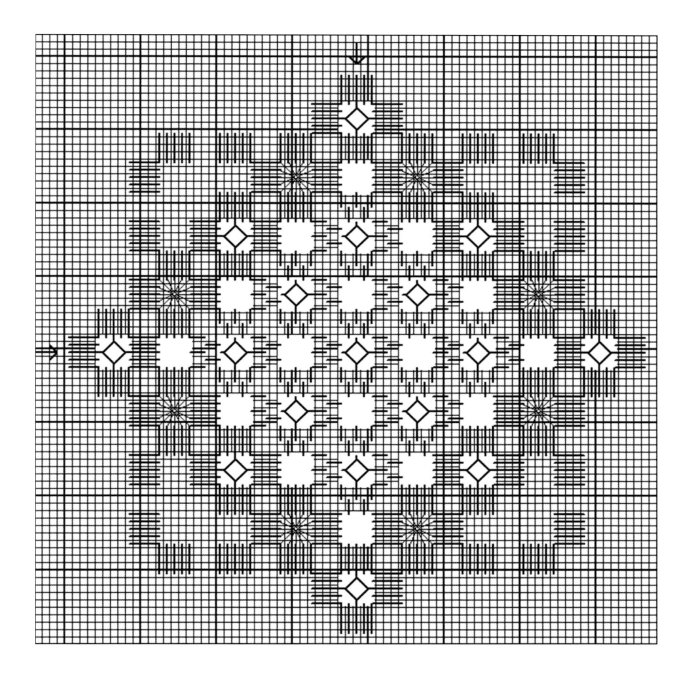

Diagram 2

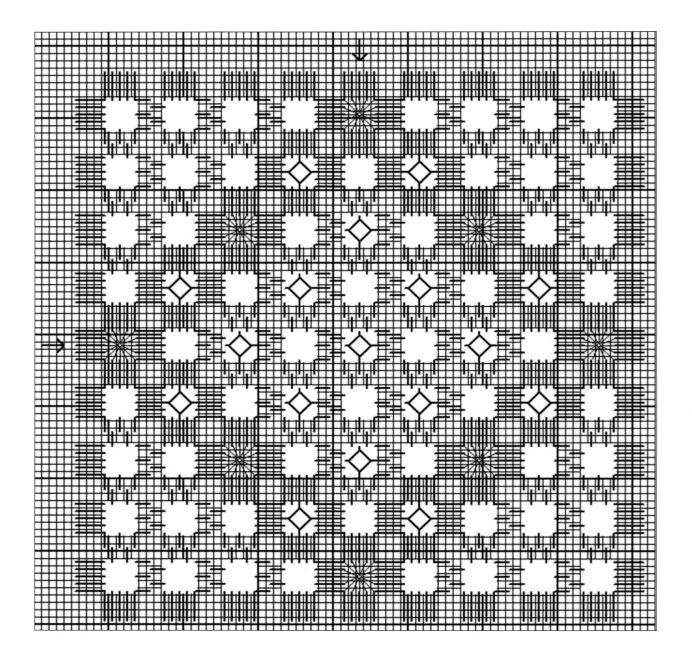

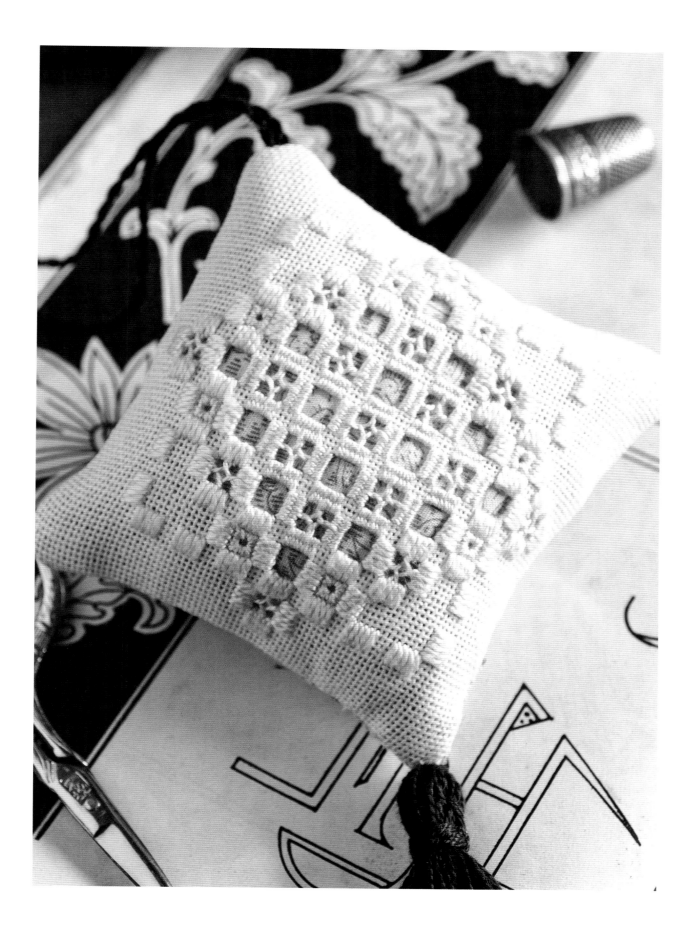

Sewing Kit

Materials

For the Hardanger

32 ct Murano fabric 3" x 8" (7 x 20 cm), color no. 530 (Sky Blue)

DMC Pearl cotton sizes 8 and 12, color no. 3753

Size 24 and 26 tapestry needles

Embroidery hoop

To assemble the kit

Dark blue quilting fabric: 8" x 44" (20 x 110 cm)

Medium blue quilting fabric: 8" x 44" (20 x 110 cm)

Light blue quilting fabric: 8" x 44" (20 x 110 cm)

1 piece of matching felt, 2½" x 5" or 2" x 4" (6 x 12 cm or 5 x 10 cm), depending on the size desired

Lightweight batting: 8" x 13¼" (20 x 33.5 cm)

1 silver magnetic snap closure

4 small metal rings

1½ yards (1.5 m) of matching bias tape or bias-cut strips from one of the fabrics: 10" (25 cm) to hold the rings and 1¼ yards for the edging

Prepare the cuts of fabric as follows:

• Fabric piece no. 1, dark blue quilting fabric: one 3" x 8" (7 x 20 cm) piece to line the embroidered Murano (includes ¼", or 0.5 cm, seam)

• Fabric piece no. 2, medium blue quilting fabric: one 8" x 11" (20 x 27.5 cm) piece for the outside of the kit (includes ¼", or 0.5 cm, seam)

• Fabric piece no. 3, medium blue quilting fabric: one 8" x 13¼" (20 x 33.5 cm) piece for the inside of the kit (includes ¼", or 0.5 cm, seam)

• Fabric piece no. 4, light blue quilting fabric: one 3⅛" x 9" (8 x 23 cm) piece for the inside pocket of the kit (includes ½", or 1 cm, seam)

• Fabric piece no. 5, dark blue quilting fabric: one 4¼" x 9" (11 x 23 cm) piece for the inside pocket of the kit (includes ½", or 1 cm, seam)

• Fabric piece no. 6, dark blue quilting fabric: two 2½" x 2½" (6 x 6 cm) pieces for the pin cushion (includes ¼", or ½ cm, seam)

Stitches used

Satin Stitch (Lesson 1)

Woven Bars (Lesson 4)

Wrapped Bars over 2 threads (Lesson 3B)

Clover Filling Stitch (Lesson 33)

Edelweiss (Lesson 27)

Flower Filling Stitch (Lesson 36)

The finished motif is 5½" x 1" (14 x 2.5 cm).

Instructions

Take the Murano fabric, and pull a thread to mark out a 3" x 8" (7 x 20 cm) rectangle. Find the center by folding the fabric in half one way and then the other. Work the satin stitches, cut and remove the threads, then work the woven and wrapped bars and the filling stitches.

When the motif is finished, follow these steps to assemble the kit:

Cut the Murano fabric following the thread previously drawn.

Sew fabric piece no. 1 to the back of the embroidery piece with a zigzag stitch around the edge (with the wrong side of the embroidery against the right side of the lining fabric).

Sew the longer side of the lined piece of embroidery to fabric no. 2 (with a ¼", or 0.5 cm, seam). The embroidered piece will become the flap of the sewing kit. Open the seam.

Using a zigzag stitch, sew the whole piece to the batting. Round off the four corners if you wish. Set aside.

Now, prepare the inside of the kit. Zigzag around the edge of fabric no. 3, then fold it into thirds and press to mark the middle of the kit and the front flap.

Make the inside pockets of the kit. Sew the longer sides of fabrics 4 and 5 together, with right sides facing each other, ½" (1 cm) from the edge. Turn right side out and press. Fabric no. 5 will become the inside of the pocket and will also act as the top edging.

Position the bottom of this pocket along the fold line previously made with the iron one-third of the way from the bottom of the fabric (right side of fabric 4 to right side of fabric 3), 4" (10 cm) from the edge. Pin, making some pleats. Sew with a seam allowance of ¼" (0.75 cm). Turn up so front of pocket faces up. Divide the pocket into 4 individual little pockets using a running stitch with the size 8 pearl cotton used for the Hardanger.

Take the 10" (25 cm) bias tape or fabric strip, fold it in half lengthwise, and topstitch close to the edge. Cut into 4 equal pieces and slide each one through a metal ring. Position them along the inside edge of the flap (meaning the edge where the embroidery is on the outside), spaced evenly and about 1" (3 cm) from the outside edges, and pin in place. They will be used to hold embroidery thread.

Make a small pin cushion from fabric piece no. 6 (with a ¼", or 0.5 cm, seam). Use whipstitch to attach it on the right or left side of the bottom third of the kit, below the 4 little pockets.

Cut one or 2 pieces of felt with pinking shears to make the needle-holder. Place it to the side of the pin cushion. Attach to the sewing kit with running stitch using the size 8 pearl cotton.

Sew on the magnetic snap closure.

Sew together the inside and outside fabrics of the kit (wrong sides together), then sew the long bias strip all around the edge, being careful to secure the ring holders along the top edge of the sewing kit.

Key

Kloster Blocks

Woven Bars

Wrapped Bars over 2 threads

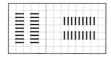

Edelweiss

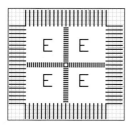

Flower Filling Stitch

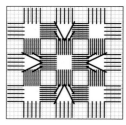

Clover Filling Stitch

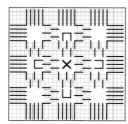

Diagram

The arrows indicate the center of the piece.

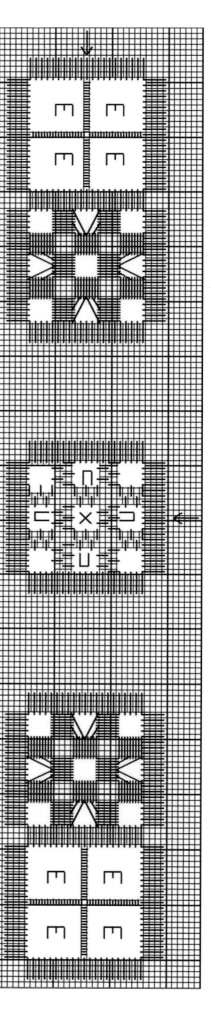

Small Bags

Materials

Blue bag

25 ct Lugana fabric, blue, 6" x 16" (15 x 40 cm), color no. 501(Wedgewood)

Marion pearl cotton sizes 5 and 8, color "Myosotis" (Forget-me-not)

Size 22 and 24 tapestry needles

Embroidery hoop

Quilting fabric for the lining: 6" x 16" (15 x 40 cm)

20" (50 cm) length of matching ¼" (6 cm) satin ribbon

Ribbon

Yellow bag

25 ct Lugana fabric, yellow, 6" x 16" (15 x 40 cm), color no. 205

Marion pearl cotton sizes 5 and 8, color "Genêt" (Broom Bush)

Size 22 and 24 tapestry needles

Embroidery hoop

2½" (6 cm) length of matching ⅛" (3mm) satin ribbon

Quilting fabric for the lining: 6" x 16" (15 x 40 cm)

Button

The finished motifs measure 3½" x 4" (9 x 10 cm) for each front side without the edge stitching.

Stitches used

Satin Stitch (Lesson 1)
Wrapped Bars over 2 threads (Lesson 3B)
Wrapped Bars over 4 threads (Lesson 3A)
Woven Bars (Lesson 4)
Eyelet Stitch (Lesson 6B)
Greek Cross (Lesson 14)
Scandinavian Four-Sided Stitch Edging (Lesson 10C)
Ladder Hemstitch (Lesson 39)

Instructions

Fold the fabric in half to mark the two sides of the bag. On one side, work the satin stitch kloster blocks around the 5 diamonds. Start with the bottom ones, ¾" (2 cm) from the fold. Place them to the right and left of the arrow indicating the center, 22 fabric threads from either side of the arrow.

Cut and remove the threads, then work the woven or wrapped bars in the 4 outside diamonds.

Next make the center diamond. Work the satin stitches on the inside, then the eyelet stitches. Cut and remove the threads and stitch the Greek cross.

Blue bag

At 24 fabric threads from the top of the diamonds, cut and pull out 4 fabric threads from side to side on the front and back, then embroider in ladder hemstitch.

At 24 fabric threads from the ladder hemstitch, finish the top edge with the Scandinavian four-sided stitch on both sides of the piece.

Line the embroidered piece, then sew the sides of the bag together. Gather the top with a little ribbon woven through the ladder hemstitch.

Yellow bag

At 52 fabric threads from the top of the diamonds, finish the top edge of the bag with the Scandinavian four-sided stitch on both sides of the piece.

Line the embroidered piece, then sew the sides of the bag together. Attach a loop of thin ribbon on one side of the top edge to fasten over a button on the other side.

Key

Kloster Blocks

Wrapped Bars over 2 threads

Greek Cross

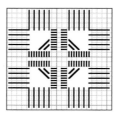

Woven Bars

Wrapped Bars over 4 threads

Eyelet Stitch

Diagram for Blue Bag
The arrows indicate the center of the design.

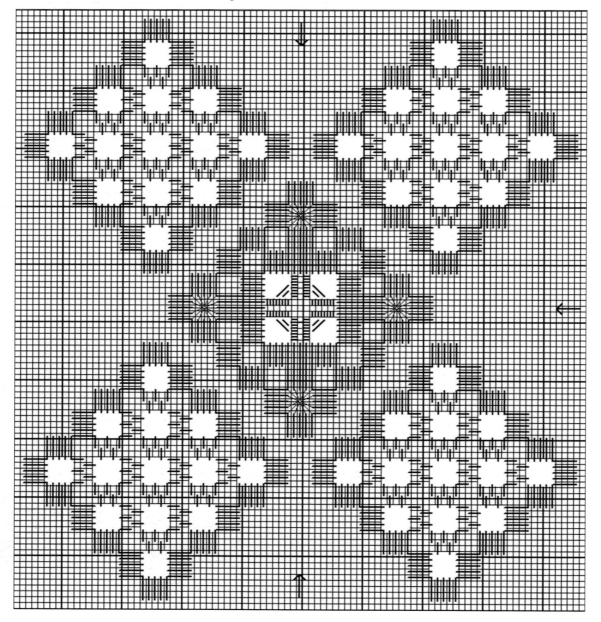

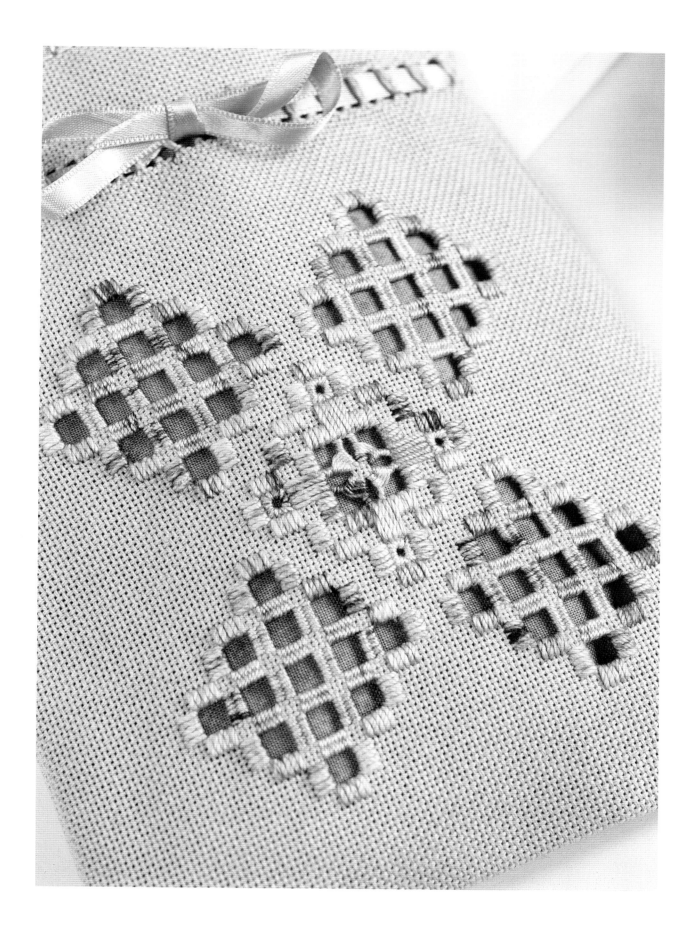

Diagram for Yellow Bag

The arrows indicate the center of the design.

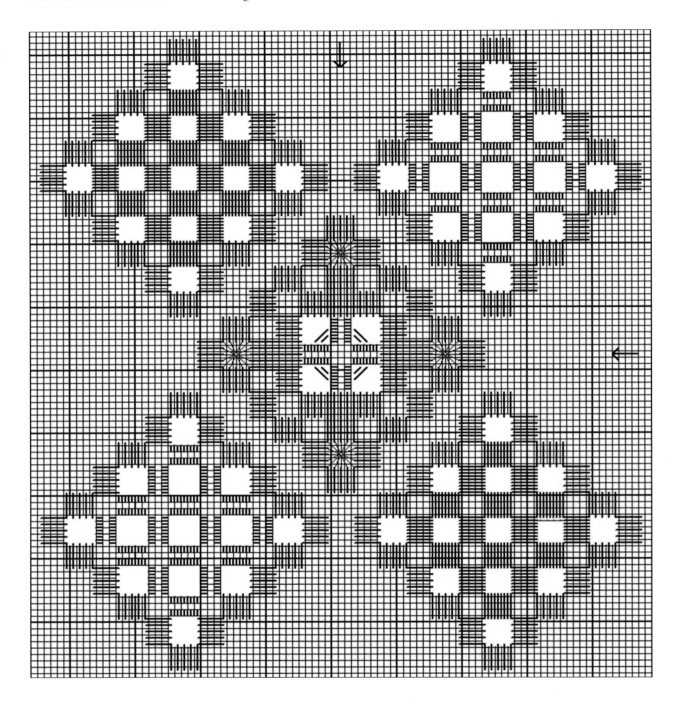

Double Heart Wedding Ring Pillow

Materials

25 ct Lugana fabric, 9½" x 9½" (24 x 24 cm), color no. 264 (Ivory)

DMC pearl cotton sizes 5 and 8, color no. 814 and ivory

Sizes 22 and 24 tapestry needles

Embroidery hoop

20" (50 cm) length of ⅛" (3 mm) garnet satin ribbon for the wedding band ties

Two pieces of quilting fabric or sateen for the lining: 9½" x 9½" (24 x 24 cm) (includes ½", or 1 cm, seam)

Fiberfill

Stitches used

Satin Stitch (Lesson 1)

Woven Bars (Lesson 4)

Dove's Eye Filling Stitch (Lesson 7)

Eyelet Stitch (Lesson 6B)

Cross Stitch (Lesson 11)

Backstitch (Lesson 13F)

The finished motif measures 8" x 8" (20 x 20 cm). The size of the pillow is 8¾" x 8¾" (22 x 22 cm).

Instructions

Find the center of the fabric by folding it in half one way and then the other.

Begin by working the satin stitch kloster blocks in the two hearts using size 5 pearl cotton in color no. 814.

Then work the rows of hearts in the same color. Backstitch the date at the bottom using size 8 pearl cotton.

In the main heart, use size 8 pearl cotton in color no. 814 to cross stitch and backstitch the initials. Work the dove's eye filling stitch with size 8 pearl cotton in ivory.

In the second heart, work the woven bars and the eyelet stitch with size 8 pearl cotton in ivory.

Sew on two 10" (25 cm) ribbon ties for the wedding bands, one at the top right of the hearts, and the other at the bottom left.

Line the piece of embroidery with one of the pieces of lining fabric (right side of lining against wrong side of embroidery), using a zigzag stitch.

Finally, assemble the lined embroidery and the second piece of lining fabric into a little pillow. Stuff with fiberfill.

Key

Kloster Blocks

Eyelet Stitch

Woven Bars

Dove's Eye Filling Stitch

Backstitch
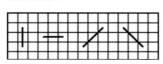

Cross Stitch

Diagram of Complete Design
Entire motif

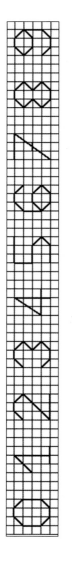

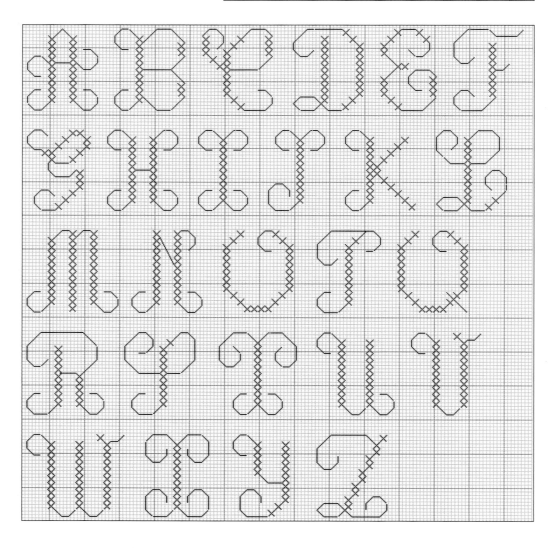

Diagrams

Center hearts and right and left borders. The small X indicates the center of the design.

The boxes indicate where the letters are to be placed.

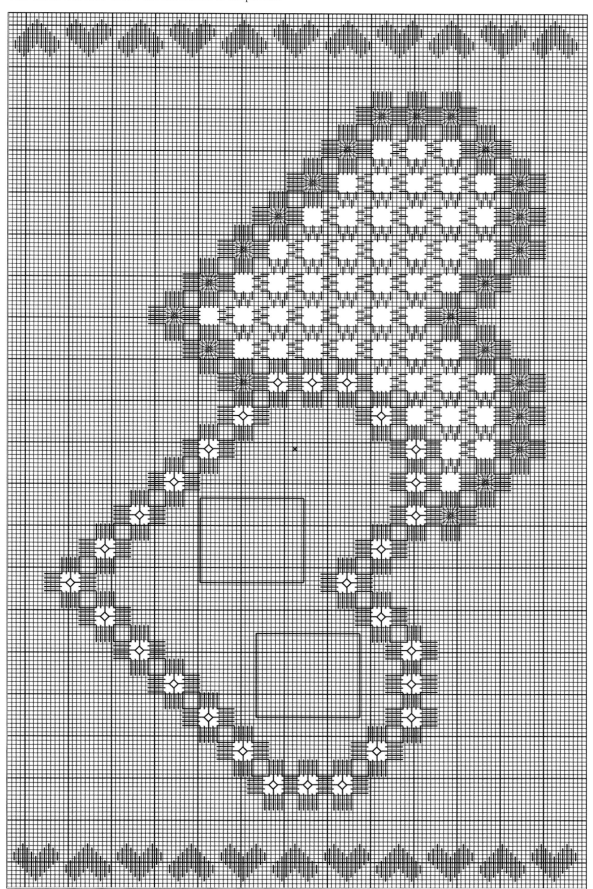

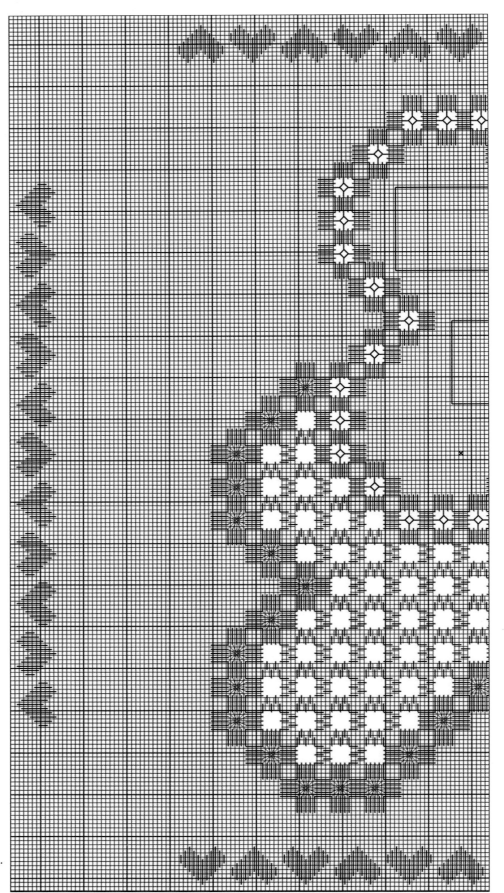

Top portion of the design.

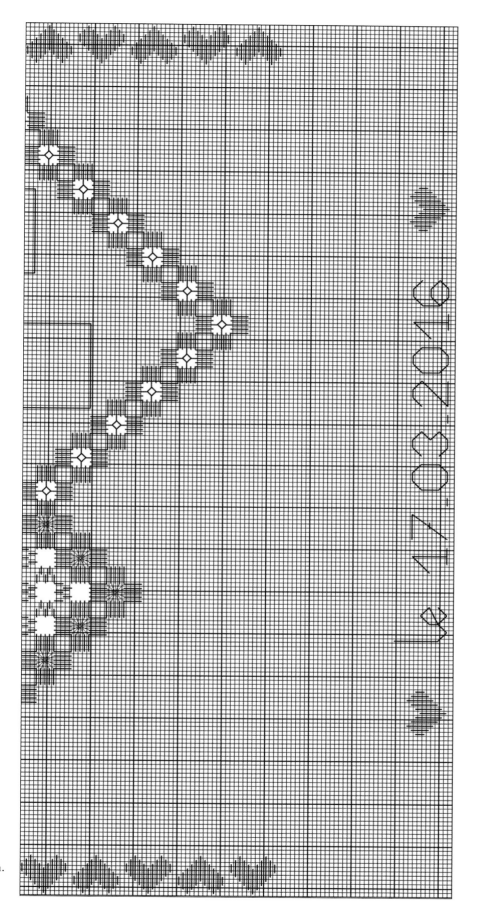

Bottom portion of the design.

Wedding Ring Pillow

Materials

25 ct Lugana fabric, 24 x 24 cm, color no. 101
  (Antique White)
DMC pearl cotton size 5, color no. 225, and size 8,
  color no. 223
Size 22 and 24 tapestry needles
Embroidery hoop
20" (50 cm) length of ⅛" (3 mm) pink satin ribbon
Two pieces of quilting fabric or sateen for the lining,
  9½" x 9½" (24 x 24 cm) (includes ½" or 1 cm seam)
Fiberfill

Stitches used

Satin Stitch (Lesson 1)
Woven Bars (Lesson 4)
Dove's Eye Filling Stitch (Lesson 7)
Cross Stitch (Lesson 11)
Backstitch (Lesson 13F)

The finished motif measures 7¼" x 7¼" (18.5 x 18.5 cm), and the size of the pillow is 8¾" x 8¾" (22 x 22 cm).

Instructions

Find the center of the fabric by folding it in half one way and then the other.

Begin by working the satin stitches using pearl cotton size 5 in color no. 225.

Cut and remove the threads, then work the woven bars and the dove's eye filling stitches with pearl cotton size 8 in color no. 223.

The date is worked in backstitch using size 8 pearl cotton in color no. 223; the initials are worked in backstitch and cross stitch using size 8 pearl cotton in color no. 223.

Sew on two 10" (25 cm) ribbon ties for the wedding bands, one in the top right corner and the other on the left between the two letters.

Line the piece of embroidery with one of the pieces of lining fabric (right side of lining against back side of embroidery), using a zigzag stitch.

Finally, assemble the lined embroidery and the second piece of lining fabric into a pillow. Stuff with fiberfill.

You will find the alphabet and number charts on page 118.

Key

Kloster Blocks

Woven Bars

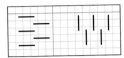

Dove's Eye Filling Stitch

Cross Stitch

Backstitch

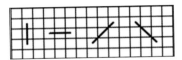

Diagram

38 THREADS

17.03.2016

Blue Pillow

Materials
25 ct Lugana fabric, 15¾" x 15¾" (40 x 40 cm), color
no. 501 (Wedgewood)
DMC pearl cotton sizes 5 and 8, color no. 3042, and
Caron cotton, ref. Pebbles
Sizes 22 and 24 tapestry needles
Embroidery hoop
Two pieces of quilting fabric or sateen for the lining,
13" x 13" (33 x 33 cm)
Fiberfill

Stitches used
Satin Stitch (Lesson 1)
Woven Bars (Lesson 4)
Star Stitch (Lesson 6)
Variations on the Cable Stitch (Lesson 13)
Rosette Stitch (Lesson 18)
Woven Inset (Lesson 21)
Single Ringed Backstitch (Lesson 17)
Diagonal Twisted Bars with Center Rosette (Lesson
15B)
Laticework (Lesson 19)
Scandinavian Four-Sided Stitch Band (Lesson 10B)

*The finished motif measures 10¾" x 10¾" (27.2 x 27.2
cm) and the size of the pillow is 13" x 13" (33 x 33 cm).*

Instructions

Begin by finding the center of the fabric by folding it in half one way and then the other.

Work cable stitch around the edges of the blocks, as indicated on the diagrams.

Then work diagonal cable stitch and the rosette stitch in the diagram 1 blocks.

Work the satin stitches and kloster blocks in the diagram 2 blocks, then cut and remove threads where necessary. Work the various decorative stitches suggested.

Finally, work the Scandinavian four-sided stitch band using size 5 pearl cotton. Start by counting 36 fabric threads from the outside cable stitch and pull the next 4 fabric threads all along each side. Weave the threads back into the corners and secure them with two kloster blocks on each corner. Work the outside stitches of the band, then the inside ones.

Line the embroidery with one of the lining fabrics using a zigzag stitch (right side of lining facing wrong side of embroidery).

Lastly, assemble the lined embroidered piece and the second lining fabric into a pillow. Stuff with fiberfill.

Key

Scandinavian Four-Sided Stitch Band

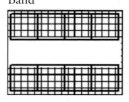

Kloster Blocks

Woven Bars

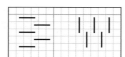

Star Stitch

Pulled Thread Work Motif

Variations on the Cable Stitch

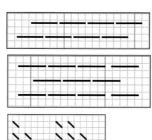

Rosette Stitch

Single Ringed Backstitch

Diagonal Twisted Bars with Center Rosette

Woven Inset

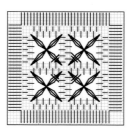

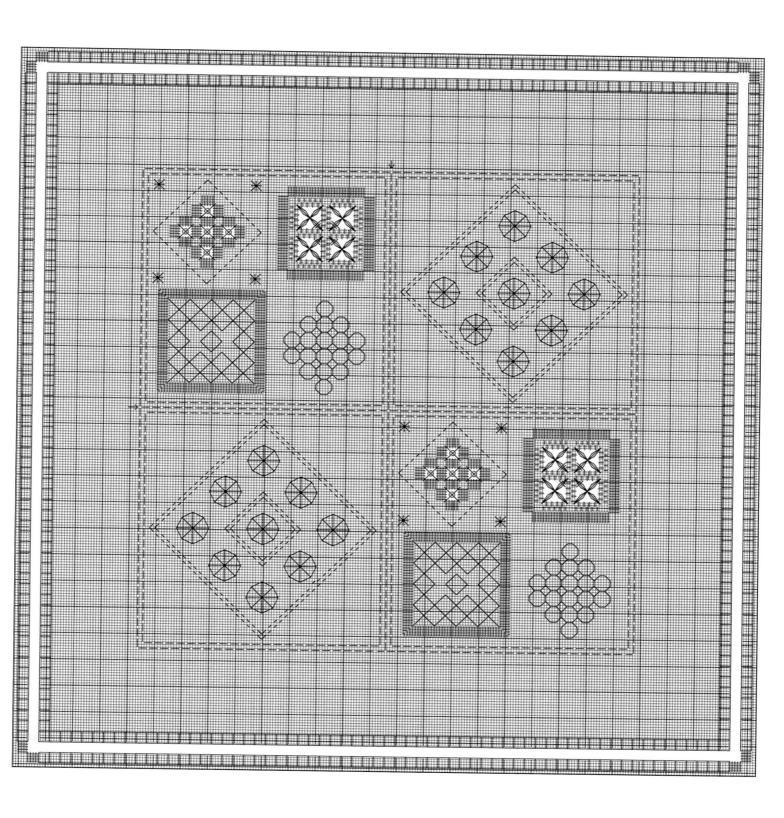

Diagram 1

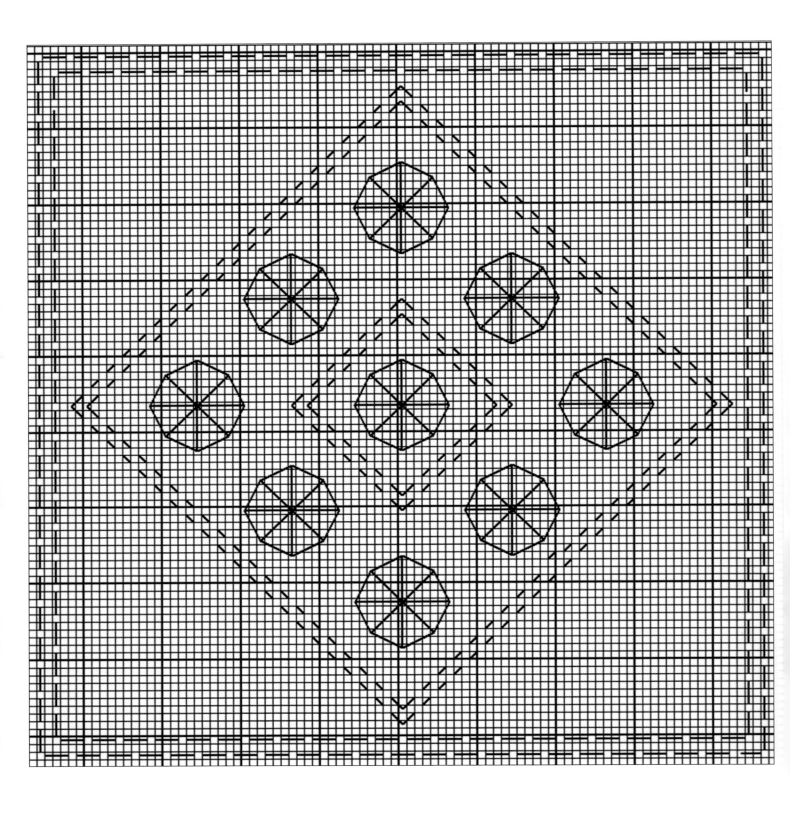

Diagram 2

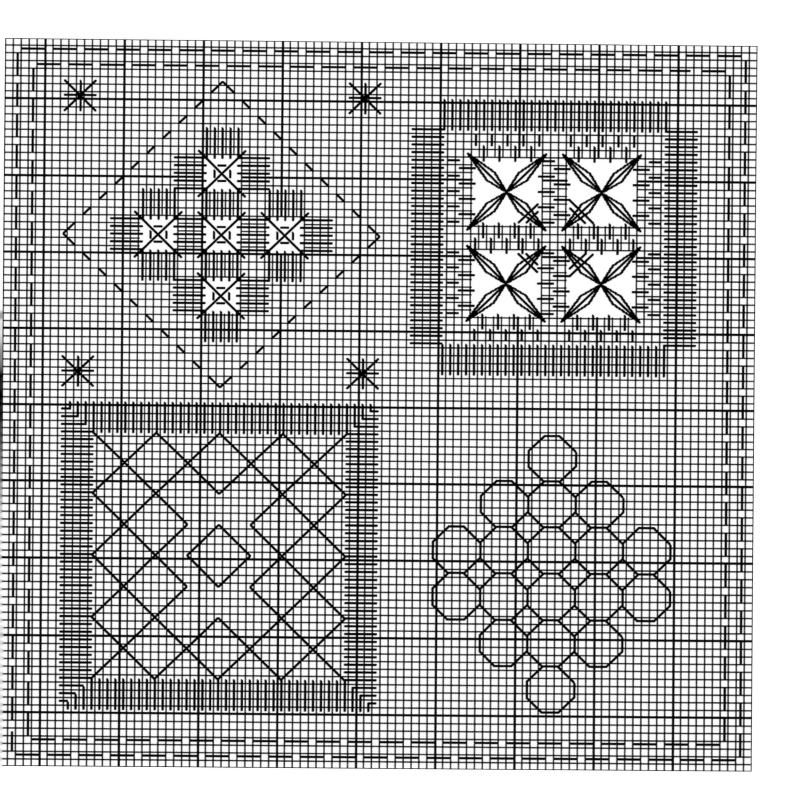

Diagram 3
Upper left corner, showing Scandinavian four-sided stitch band.

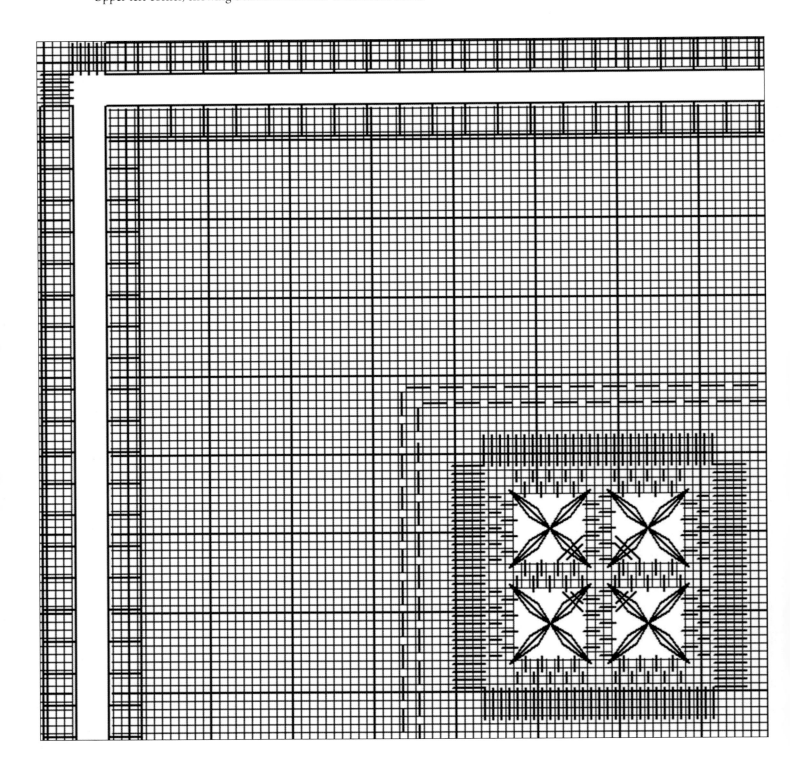

Triangle Pillow

Materials

25 ct Lugana fabric, 21¾" x 17¾" (55 x 45 cm), color no. 274 (Baby Yellow)
DMC Pearl cotton sizes 5 and 8, color no. 92
Sizes 22 and 24 tapestry needles
Embroidery hoop
Two pieces of quilting fabric or sateen for the lining: 21¾" x 17¾" (55 x 45 cm)
Fiberfill
2 tassels

Stitches used

Satin Stitch (Lesson 1)
Woven Bars (Lesson 4)
Dove's Eye Filling Stitch (Lesson 7)
Square Filet Filling Stitch (Lesson 7C)

The finished work measures 19¼" x 14½" (49 x 37 cm).

Instructions

Find the center of the fabric by folding it in half one way and then the other.

Refer to diagram 2 to determine the placement of the various diamonds and diagram 1 for the details of the stitches.

Work the kloster blocks, cut and remove the threads, and then complete the other stitches.

Draw a triangle that will easily encompass the embroidery, and copy it onto the 3 fabrics. Cut out the pieces.

Use a zigzag stitch to attach one of the lining fabrics to the back of the embroidery (right side of lining facing wrong side of embroidery).

Lastly, assemble the pillow and stuff with fiberfill. Remember to insert the two tassels in two corners.

Key

Kloster Blocks

Woven Bars

Square Filet Filling Stitch

Dove's Eye Filling Stitch

Diagram 1
Embroider the 3 points with the motif shown below.

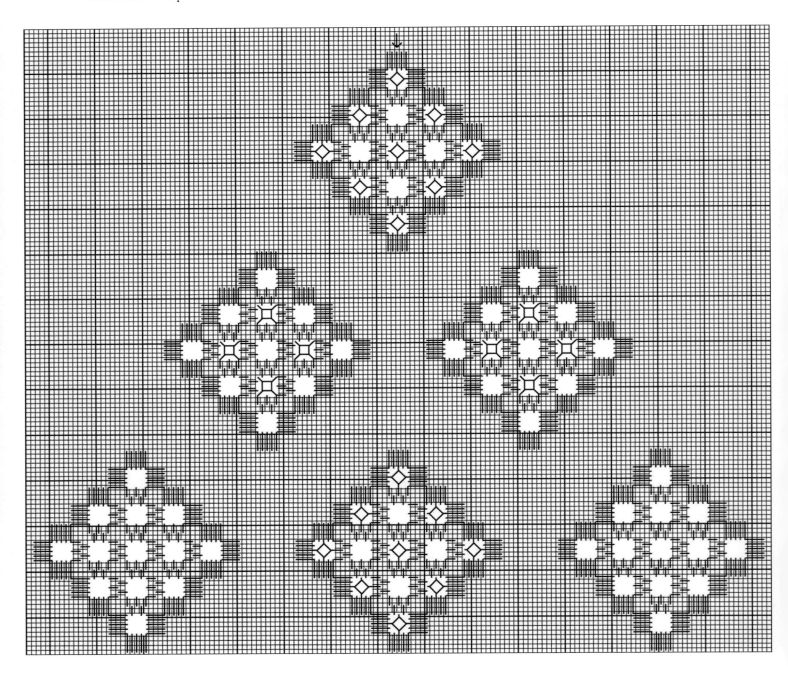

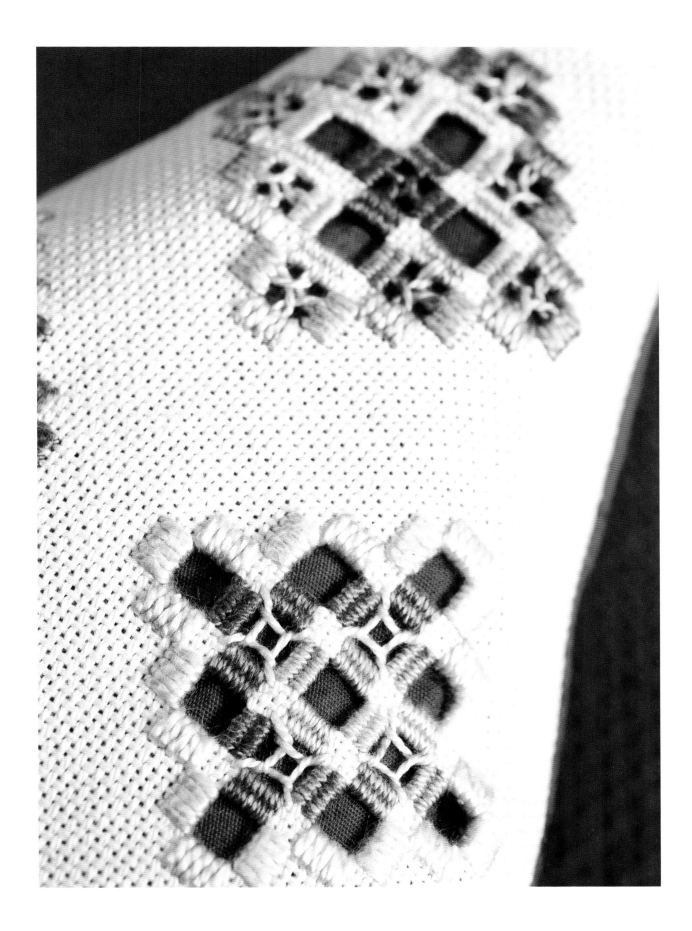

Diagram 2

The 3 diamonds are the bottom row of the top corner of the triangle. The 2 diamonds at the left and the right are the top points of the 2 lower triangle corners. The X at the end of the arrow marked "22 threads" is the center of the design.

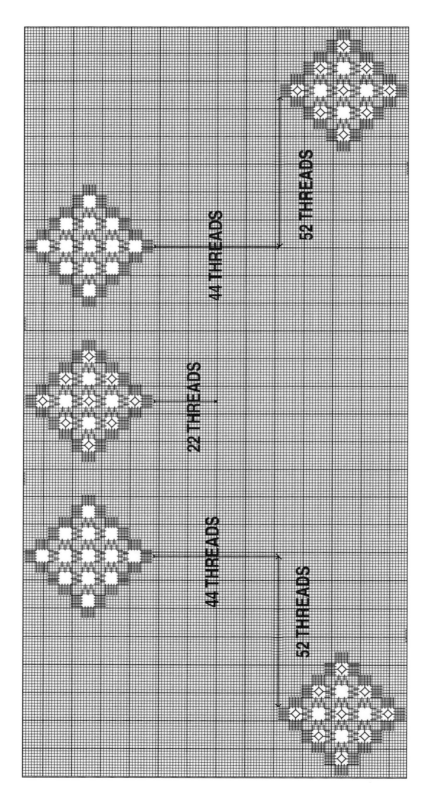

Octagonal Mat

Materials

25 ct Lugana fabric, 12½" x 12½" (32 x 32 cm), color no. 264 (Ivory)
DMC Pearl cotton sizes 5 and 8, color no. 712
Size 22 and 24 tapestry needles
Embroidery hoop

Stitches used

Satin Stitch (Lesson 1)
Tulip Motifs (Lesson 1C)
Woven Bars (Lesson 4)
Diagonal Twisted Bars (Lesson 15A)
Shuttle Stitch (Lesson 28)
Leaf (Lesson 35)
Buttonhole Stitch (Lesson 9)
Scandinavian Four-Sided Stitch (Lesson 10A)

The finished motif measures 8¾" x 8¾" (22 x 22 cm).

Instructions

Find the center of the fabric by folding it in half one way and then the other.

Work the tulip motifs in satin stitch, starting from the middle. Diagrams 2 and 3 go next to each other.

Work the kloster blocks in the 4 triangles, cut and remove the threads, work the woven bars, then work the different filling stitches.

Diagram 3 shows how the edging is to be finished. The tulip motif shown represents the last one at each of the four corners. The inside of the edging is worked in satin stitch using size 5 pearl cotton; the Scandinavian four-sided stitch is worked in the middle using size 8 pearl cotton; and a buttonhole stitch is worked along the outside edge in size 8 pearl cotton.

Key

Kloster Blocks

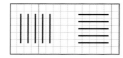

Tulip Motifs

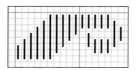

Buttonhole Stitch

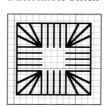

Woven Bars

Scandinavian Four-Sided Stitch

Shuttle Stitch

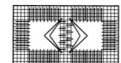

Leaf

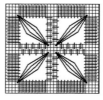

Twisted Diagonal Bars

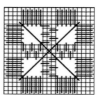

Diagram 1
Edging

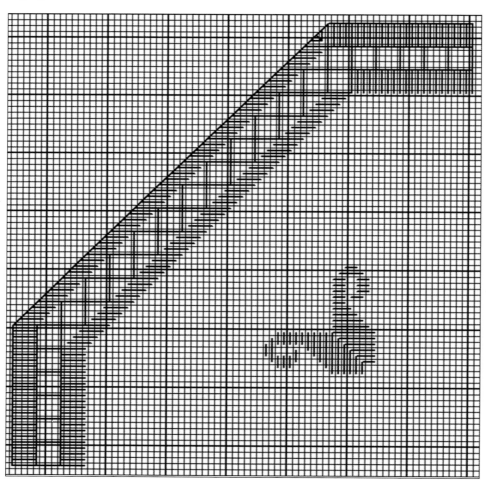

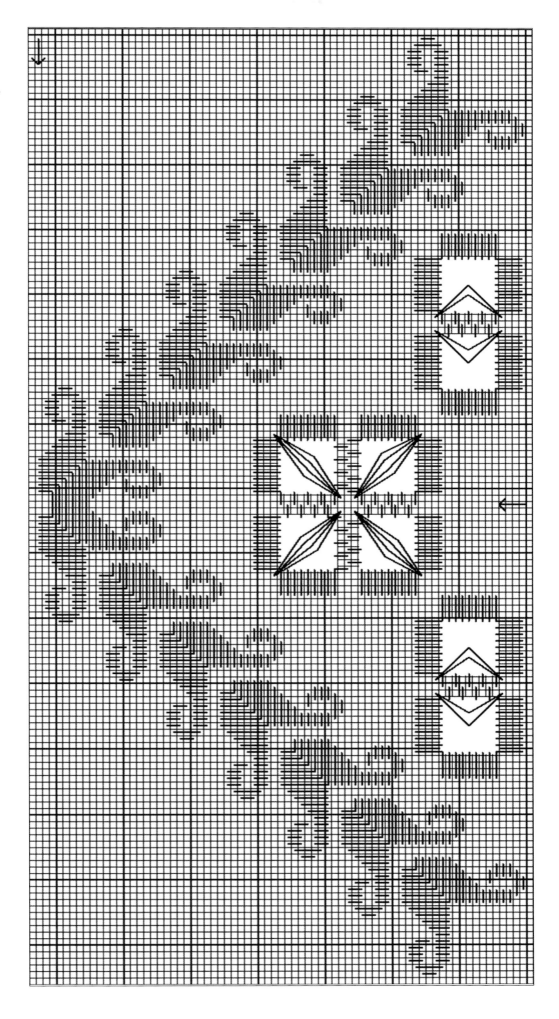

Diagram 2
Top and bottom sections of mat. The arrows indicate the center of the design.

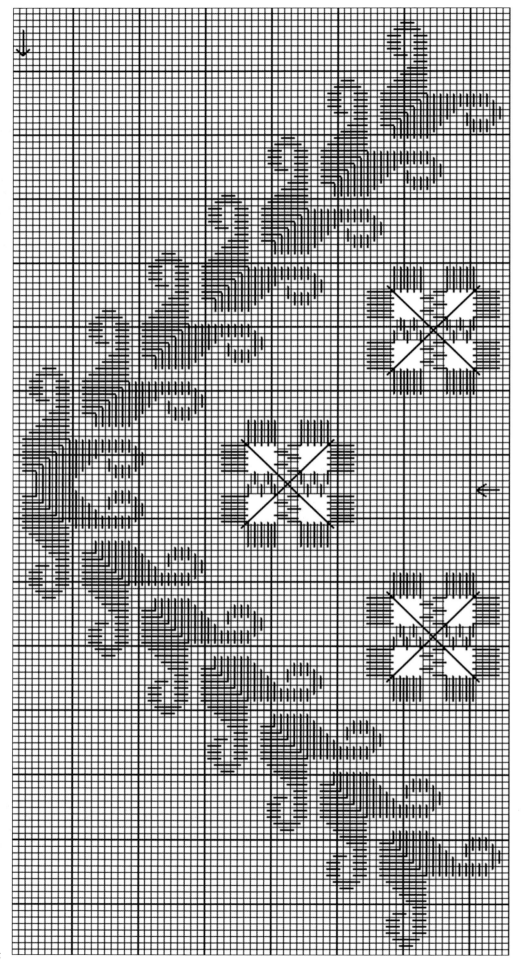

Diagram 3
Right and left sections of mat. The arrows indicate the center of the design.

Welcome Sampler

Materials

25 ct Lugana fabric, 11¾" x 27½" (30 x 70 cm), color
  no. 309 (Sand)
DMC pearl cotton sizes 5 and 8, color no. 90
Sizes 22 and 24 tapestry needles
Embroidery hoop
20" (50 cm) length of ⅛" (3mm) satin ribbon

Stitches used

Satin Stitch (Lesson 1)
Woven Bars (Lesson 4)
Diagonal Twisted Bars with Center Rosette (Spider's
  Web Filling Stitch) (Lesson 15B)
Variations on the Cable Stitch (Lesson 13)
Cross Stitch (Lesson 11)
Scandinavian Four-Sided Stitch (Lesson 10)
Spider without Openwork (Lesson 26B)
Flower Filling Stitch (Lesson 36)
Fly Stitch (Lesson 20)
Double Zigzag Hemstitch (Lesson 42)
Interlaced Hemstitch (Lesson 43)
Interlaced Crossed Ladder Hemstitch (Lesson 43C)
Ladder Hemstitch (Lesson 39)
Zigzag Hemstitch (Lesson 40)

The finished work measures 10" x 23" (25 x 58 cm).

Instructions

Find the center of the fabric by folding it in half one
way and then the other. Count the number of fabric
threads between the middle and the four-sided stitches,
then work the 2 rows of four-sided stitches.

Work the satin stitches at each end of the drawn thread
area, then cut and remove the threads. Complete the
interlacing stitch with the ribbon.

Following the diagram, complete the various motifs on
both sides of the center drawn thread work area.

Next, work the zigzag hemstitches on the right and left
sides:
• cut and remove threads from end to end
• baste a ½" (1 cm) rolled hem on the outside edge of
  each hemstitch
• work the zigzag hemstitch

Finish with the ladder hemstitches on the top and bottom:
• cut and remove threads as indicated on the diagram
• make a 1" (2.5 cm) hem on each end and baste
• embroider the ladder hemstitch, which acts as a seam
  for the hem

Slide a rod through the top pocket for hanging, and
another through the bottom, to help the sampler hang
straight, if you wish.

Key

Kloster Blocks

Woven Bars

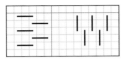

Variations on the Cable Stitch

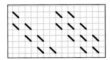

Diagonal Twisted Bars with Center Rosette

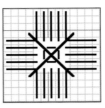

Cross Stitch

Scandinavian Four-Sided Stitch

Fly Stitch

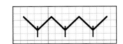

Ladder Hemstitch

Zigzag Hemstitch

Spider without openwork

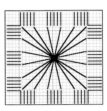

Flower Filling Stitch

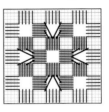

Diagrams

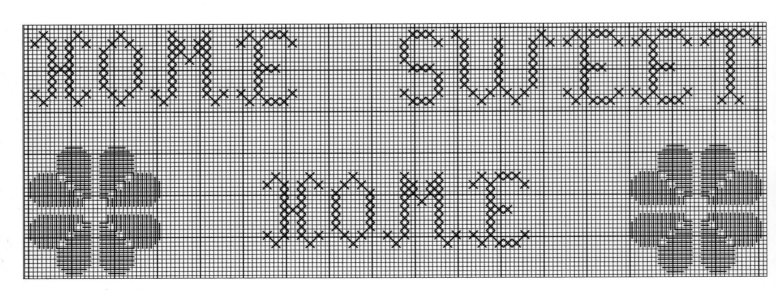

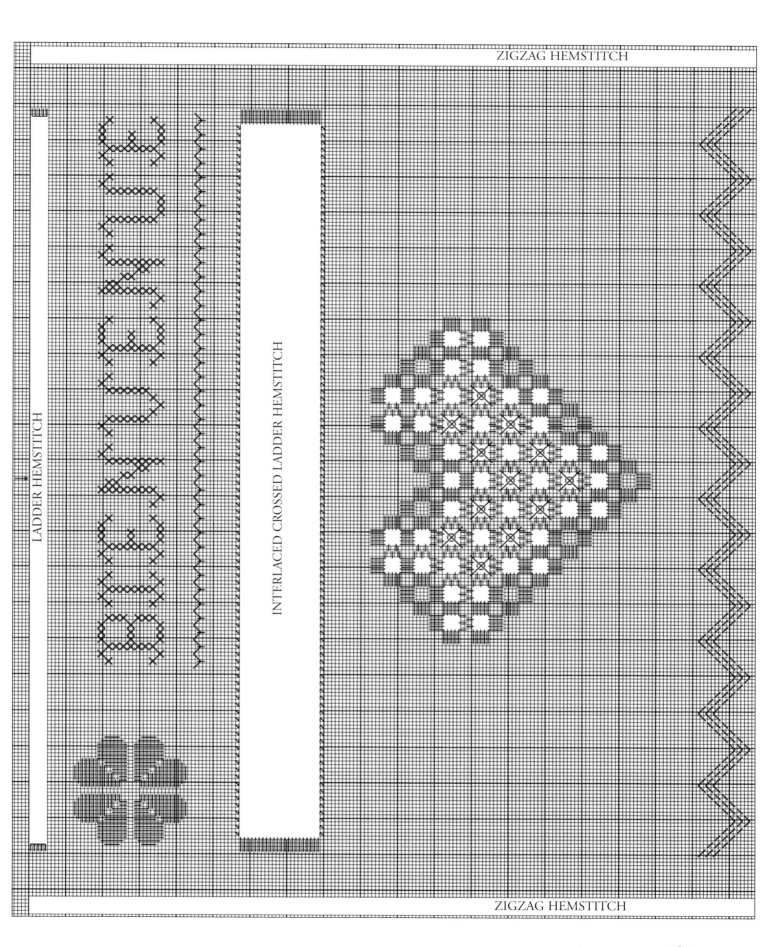

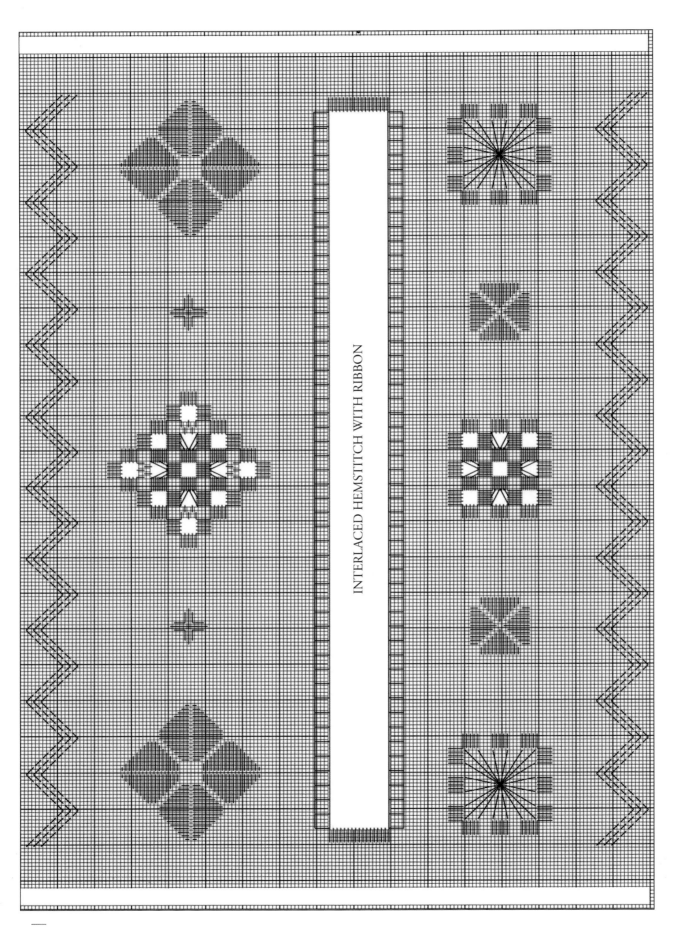

INTERLACED HEMSTITCH WITH RIBBON

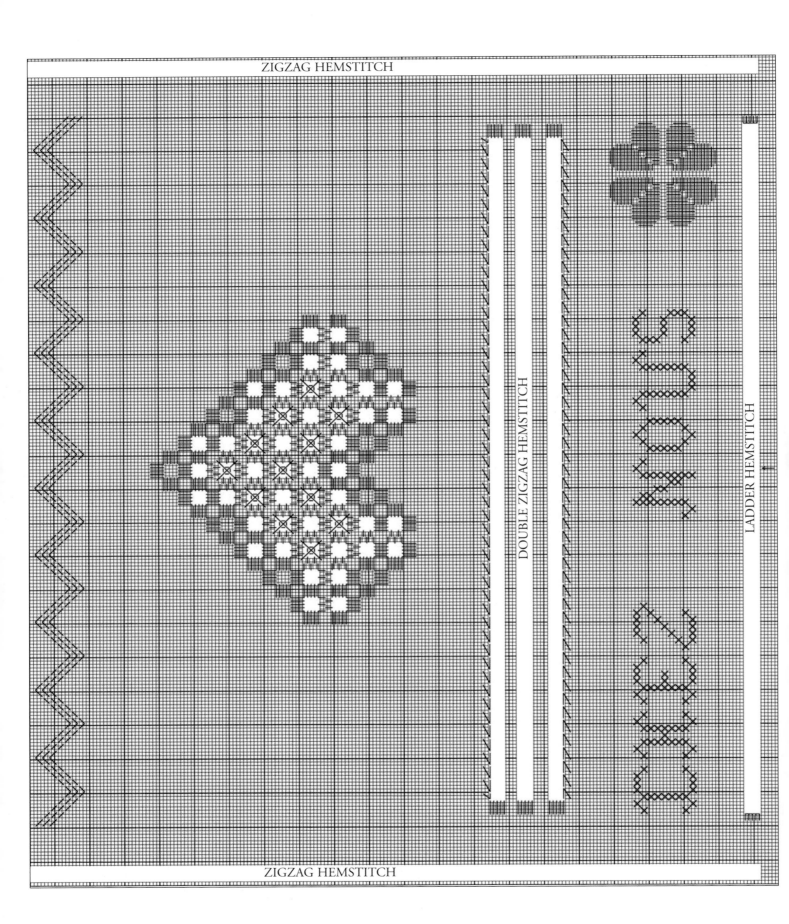

Place Mat

Materials

25 ct Lugana fabric, 21½" x 17" (55 x 43 cm), color
  no. 309 (Sand)
DMC pearl cotton sizes 5 and 8, color no. 842
Size 22 and 24 tapestry needles
Embroidery hoop

Stitches used

Satin Stitch (Lesson 1)
Wrapped Bars over 2 threads (Lesson 3B)
Edelweiss (Lesson 27)
Spider (Lesson 26A)
Greek Cross (Lesson 14)
Woven Petals (Lesson 22)
Zigzag Hemstitch (Lesson 40)
Mitered Corners (Lesson 38)

The finished motif measures 14¼" x 19" (36 x 48 cm).

Instructions

Pull a thread along each side of the fabric to obtain a piece measuring exactly 21½" x 17" (55 x 43 cm). Cut and overcast stitch along the edge.

At 2¾" (7 cm) from the edge, work the satin stitches of the top right motif. Cut and remove the threads, then work the remainder of the stitches shown.

Count 8 fabric threads from the outside of the satin stitches and pull the next 4 threads for the zigzag hemstitch. Bring them to the opposite edge. There should be about 2¾" (7 cm) of fabric border before turning. However, to be sure there is the right number of threads (meaning a multiple of 4), stitch the inside edge of the zigzag hemstitch as you are removing the threads. Do the same on all four sides. Keep in mind that the drawn threads are to be rewoven into the corners and secured with buttonhole stitches over 2 or 3 fabric threads.

Now work the satin stitches in the bottom left motif.

Cut and remove the threads, then work the remainder of the stitches shown.

Finally, prepare the second part of the zigzag hemstitch and the mitered corners. Count 20 fabric threads from the outside of the drawn thread area previously prepared and baste along that line.

From that basting line, count another 20 fabric threads outward and baste another line there.

From this second basting line, count 10 fabric threads and pull out the next thread. Cut straight along the drawn thread space. Overcast the edge.

Next, using an iron, prepare the 4 mitered corners and baste to hold them in place. Remove the basting lines no longer needed.

Work the outside edge of the zigzag hemstitch and the buttonhole stitches in the corners.

Sew the mitered corners using an invisible stitch.

Key

Kloster Blocks

Wrapped Bars over 2 threads

Greek Cross

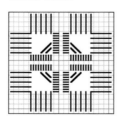

Woven Petals

Edelweiss

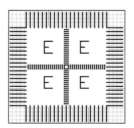

Spider

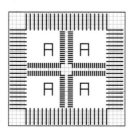

Diagram 1
Bottom left motif.

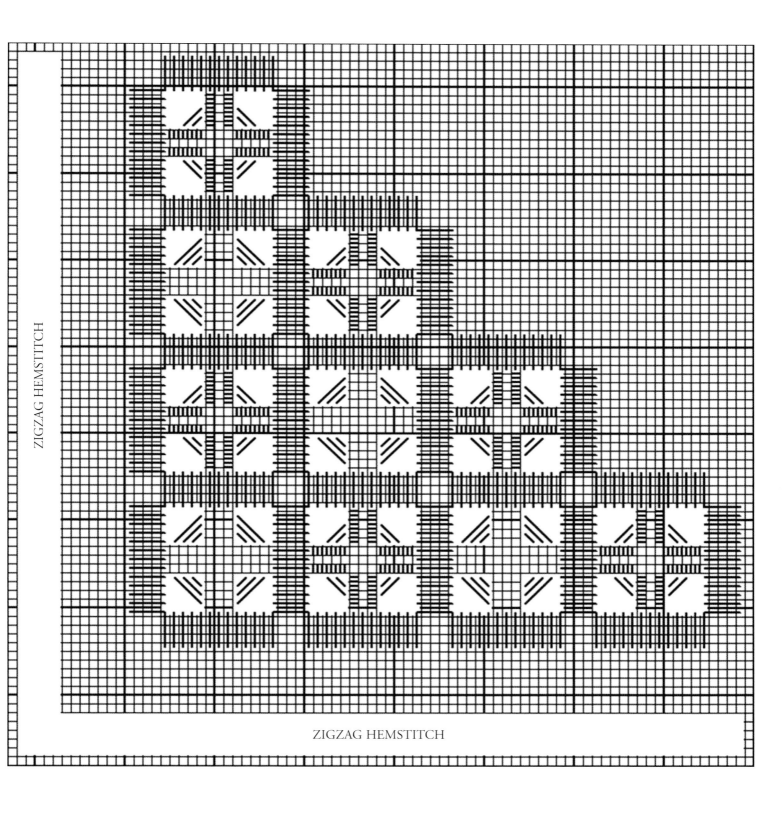

ZIGZAG HEMSTITCH

ZIGZAG HEMSTITCH

Diagram 2

Upper right motif.

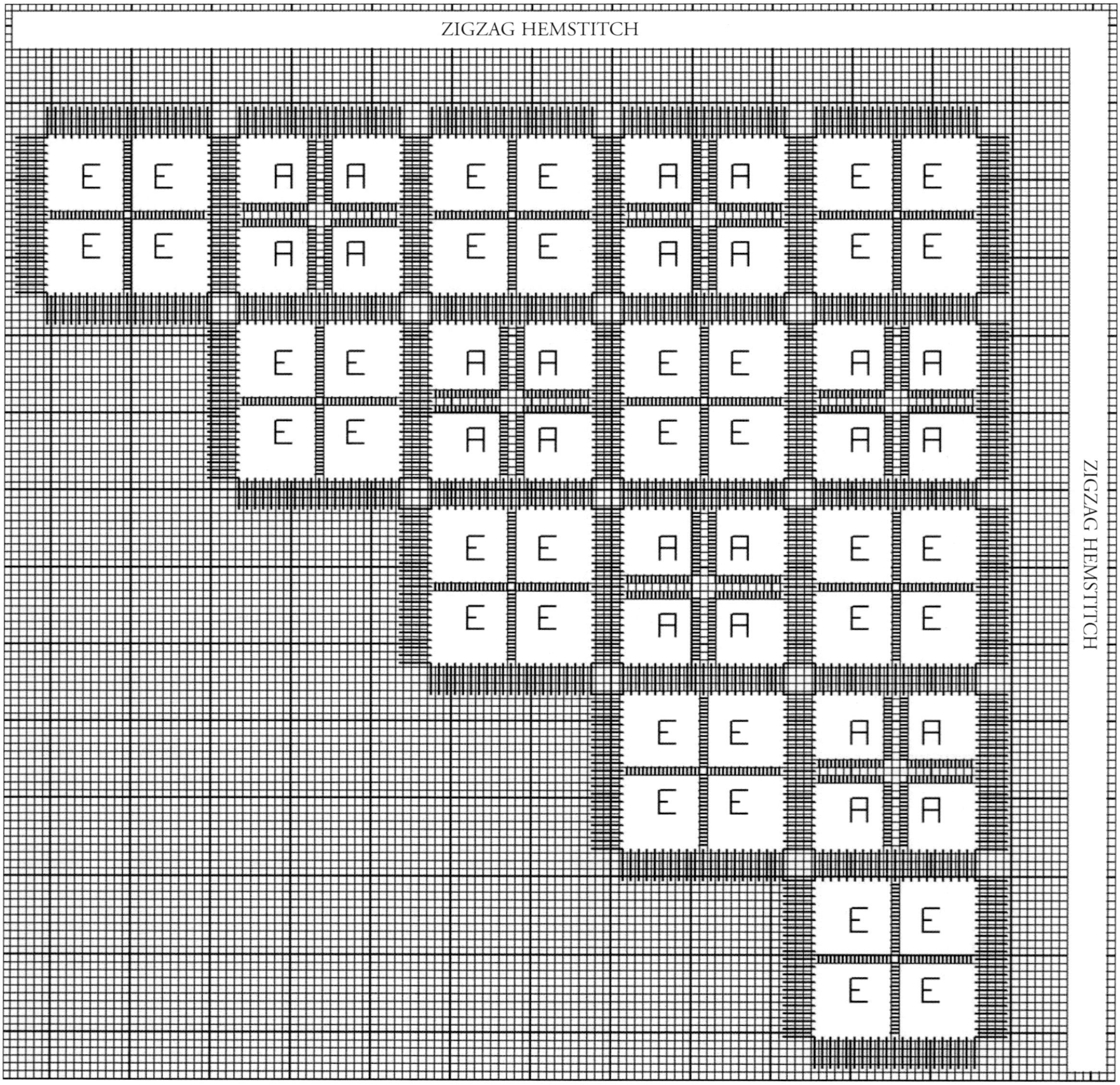

Table Runner

Materials

25 ct Lugana fabric, Fein-Floba quality, 47¼" x 17¼"
(120 x 44 cm), color no. 53 (Oatmeal)
DMC pearl cotton sizes 5 and 8, color no. 712
Size 22 and 24 tapestry needles
Embroidery hoop

Stitches used

Satin Stitch (Lesson 1)
Wrapped Bars over 2 and 4 threads (Lesson 3)
Woven Bars (Lesson 4)
Edelweiss (Lesson 27)
Uneven Woven Bars (Lesson 5)
Four-Petal Flower (Lesson 24)
Spider (Lesson 26A)
Divided Branch (Lesson 16)
Fan Stitch (Lesson 25)
Twisted Lattice Band (Lesson 12)
Variations on the Cable Stitch (Lesson 13)
Single Ringed Backstitch (Lesson 17)
Four-Sided Stitch (Lesson 10)
Ladder Hemstitch (Lesson 39)

The finished motif measures 4¼" x 15¾" (120 x 40 cm).

Instructions

Prepare a rectangle 47¼" x 17¼" (120 x 44 cm), pulling threads to be sure to obtain a straight cut. Overcast the edge. If you like, you can add basting lines for reference at this point (see Diagram 1).

Fold the fabric in half one way and then the other to find the center and begin the diamond worked in the Scandinavian four-sided stitch. The first four-sided stitch surrounds the center thread; work 25 others on each side of it to obtain a total of 51 four-sided stitches.

Continue working to the top and bottom of the center line, decreasing by one square on each end of every row. Stop when only one square remains.

Count 137 fabric threads from the left point, and then from the right point, of the Scandinavian four-sided stitch diamond. You are now at the center of block 2 on one side and block 5 on the other.

Work the kloster blocks and the twisted lattice bands of these two blocks. Cut and remove the threads. Add the decorative stitches.

Referring to drawing 2 to determine their positions, complete blocks 1, 3, 4, and 6 as above. On the drawing, the lines of the squares represent the outside edge of the twisted lattice band, and the numbers indicate the fabric threads to count in between the blocks.

Now use squares 1 and 6 as a reference point for working the triangle of single ringed backstitch at each end. Count 50 fabric threads, as shown on Diagram 2 and work 41 ringed backstitches across. Start to form the triangle by decreasing one ringed backstitch on each end of every row. Stop when you are down to one ringed backstitch. Work in the same manner on the opposite end.

For the edges, start from the points on the top and bottom of the four-sided stitch diamond (along basting line B), and count 86 fabric threads. At that point, work a horizontal double cable stitch along the edge

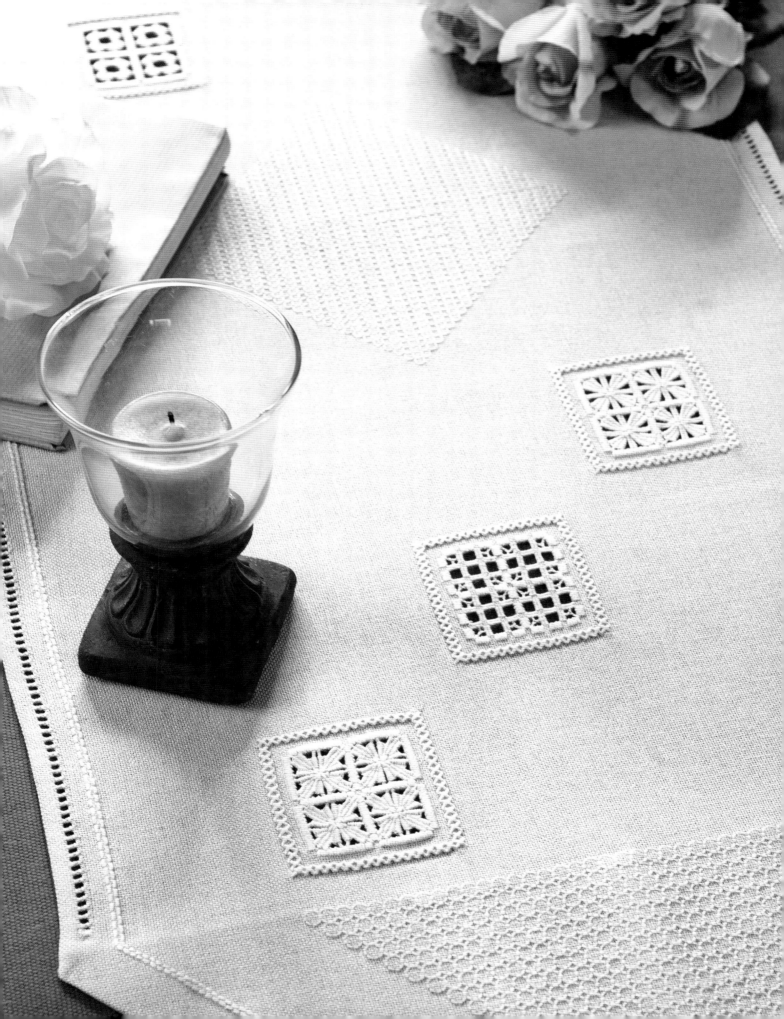

with size 5 pearl cotton. When you get to basting lines E and F, at the base of the ringed backstitch triangles, continue with the double cable stitch, but in a diagonal line. To do this, one of the horizontal stitches is made over 2 fabric threads instead of 4.

Continue to basting line A, at the point of the ringed backstitch triangle, and return diagonally on the opposite side to line E. Continue in the same manner around the remainder of the edge of the piece.

At 9 fabric threads from the outside edge of the horizontal cable stitch, pull the next four fabric threads. Fold the remaining ¾" (2 cm) of fabric between the edge of the fabric and the drawn thread area into thirds. Press and baste.

Work the ladder hemstitch over 4 fabric threads. Be careful to stop the hemstitch 10 fabric threads before basting lines E and F (at the base of the ringed backstitch triangles). There should be 183 hemstitches. Weave the ends of the pulled threads back into the fabric and work buttonhole stitches over 3 fabric threads to secure them.

To make the points, fold the fabric in half lengthwise and, with right sides together, make a seam along each end of the fabric, ⅜" (8mm) from the edge. Open the seams and press them.

Turn the piece right side out and the 2 points will appear.

Key

Kloster Blocks

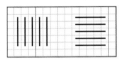

Woven Bars

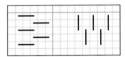

Wrapped Bars over 4 threads

Wrapped Bars over 2 threads

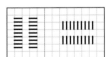

Variations on the Cable Stitch

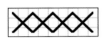

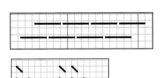

Twisted Lattice Band

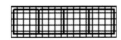

Spider

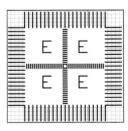

Edelweiss

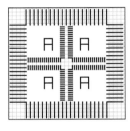

Fan Stitch

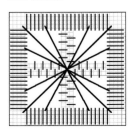

Uneven Woven Bars

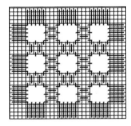

Four-Petal Flower

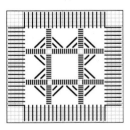

Single Ringed Backstitch

Four-Sided Stitch

Divided Branch

Diagrams of Embroidered Blocks

Diagram 1

Note that this drawing is not to scale. Lines A, B, C, D, E, and F indicate where you could place basting lines for reference. This step is optional.

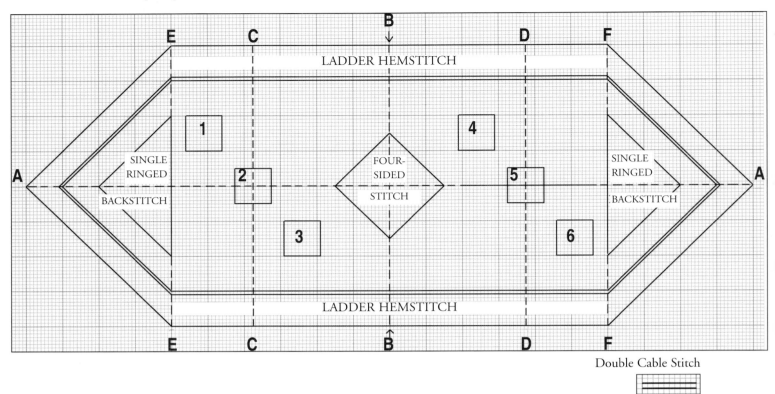

Double Cable Stitch

Diagram 2

Note that this drawing is not to scale. The lines of the squares represent the outside edge of the twisted lattice band, and the numbers indicate the threads to be counted to position the various motifs. The spacing is the same for squares 1, 2, and 3.

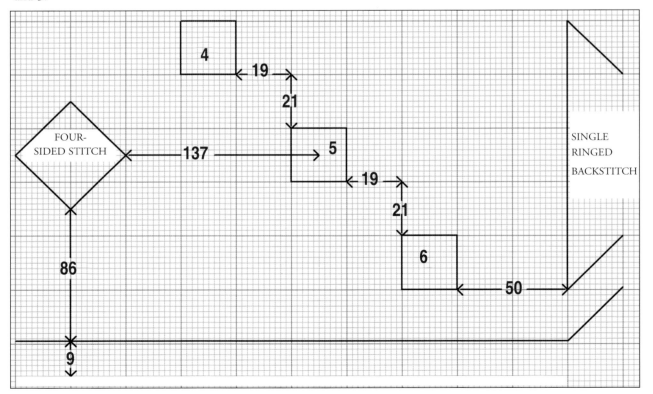

Tablecloth

Materials

25 ct Lugana fabric, 40" x 40" (100 x 100 cm), color no. 100 (White)
DMC pearl cotton sizes 5 and 8, color B5200
Size 22 and 24 tapestry needles
Embroidery hoop

Stitches used

Satin Stitch (Lesson 1)
Woven Bars (Lesson 4)
Wrapped Bars over 4 threads (Lesson 3A)
Dove's Eye Filling Stitch (Lesson 7)
Square Filet Filling Stitch (Lesson 7C)
Diagonal Triple Cable Stitch (Lesson 13E)
Venetian Wrapped Hemstitch (Lesson 41)
Zigzag Hemstitch (Lesson 40)
Drunkard's Path (Lesson 34)
Woven Flower (Lesson 32)
Ribbed Wheel (Lesson 23)
Buttonhole Stitch Circle (Lesson 30)
Clover Filling Stitch (Lesson 33)
Buttonhole Stitch Flower (Lesson 31)
Buttonhole Arch Filling Stitch (Lesson 29)
Woven Petals (Lesson 22)
Mitered Corners (Lesson 38)

The finished motif measures 34" x 34" (86.5 x 86.5 cm).

Instructions

Find the center of the fabric by folding it in half one way and then the other, then sew a basting line from end to end to use as a point of reference.

Mark off a center square 200 threads by 200 threads. Start at the center and count out 100 fabric threads and pull the 101st thread. Do the same on all four sides and the spaces from the removed threads should all meet.

Pull the following 3 fabric threads on each side, weave the ends all back into the corners, and secure them with buttonhole stitches over 2 or 3 threads.

Work the Venetian wrapped hemstitch in the drawn thread area.

Count 12 fabric threads from the Venetian wrapped hemstitch and work the kloster blocks of motifs 1, 2, 3, and 4. The center of each of the 4 motifs must be at the center of each side of the Venetian wrapped hemstitch square.

Cut and remove the threads and work the stitches indicated in the diagrams.

Next, work the 4 triple diagonal cable stitch lines, starting 2 fabric threads from the 4 corners of the Venetian wrapped hemstitch (from the corner where the buttonhole stitches meet). There should be 150 center stitches and 149 outside stitches.

Count 4 threads from the last cable stitch and cut and remove the next 4 fabric threads. The drawn threadwork area on the 4 sides will meet to form the border.

Make mitered corners. To do this, count 30 fabric threads and sew a basting line. Count another 30 threads and place another basting line. Finally, count 10 fabric threads, pull the next thread and cut the fabric along the space obtained from the removed thread. Overcast stitch around the edge, press, cut the extra fabric in the corners, and baste.

Complete the zigzag hemstitch.

Overall view

This drawing is not to scale. The numbers indicate blocks worked in that area.

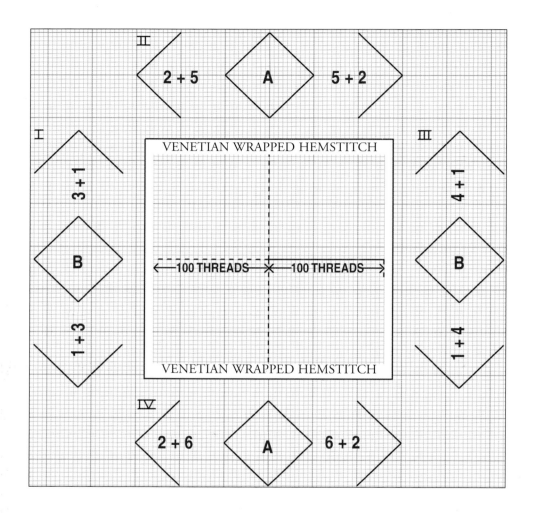

Key

Kloster Blocks

Woven Bars

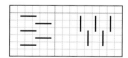

Square Filet Filling Stitch

Variations on the Cable Stitch

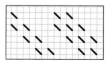

Wrapped Bars over 4 threads

Dove's Eye Filling Stitch

Diagram 1 (blocks B, 1, 3)

This diagram shows half of the motif. The other half is its mirror image.

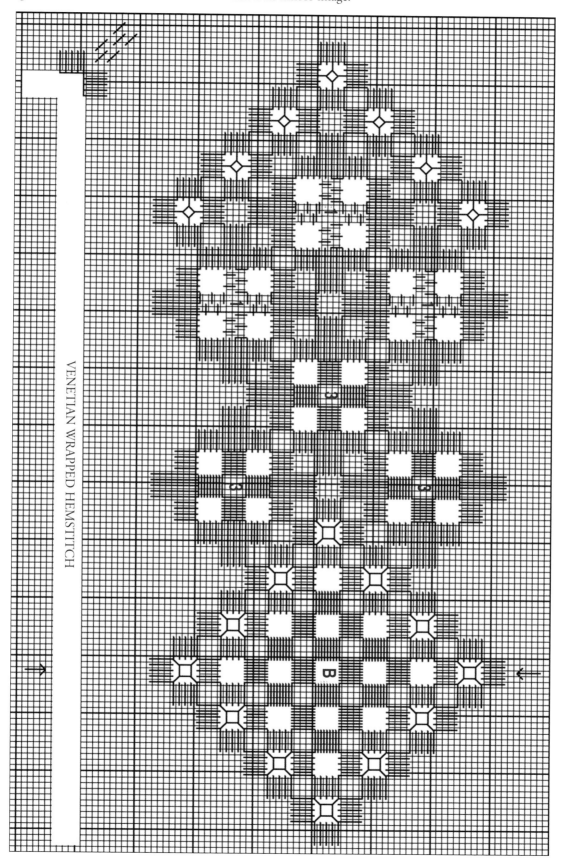

VENETIAN WRAPPED HEMSTITCH

Diagram 2 (blocks A, 2, 5)

This diagram shows half of the motif. The other half is its mirror image.

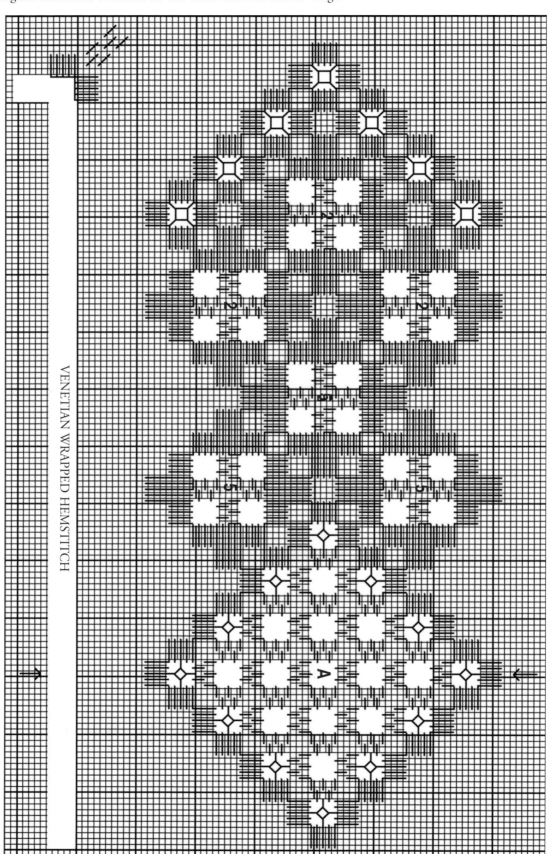

Diagram 3 (blocks B, 1, 4)

This diagram shows half of the motif. The other half is its mirror image.

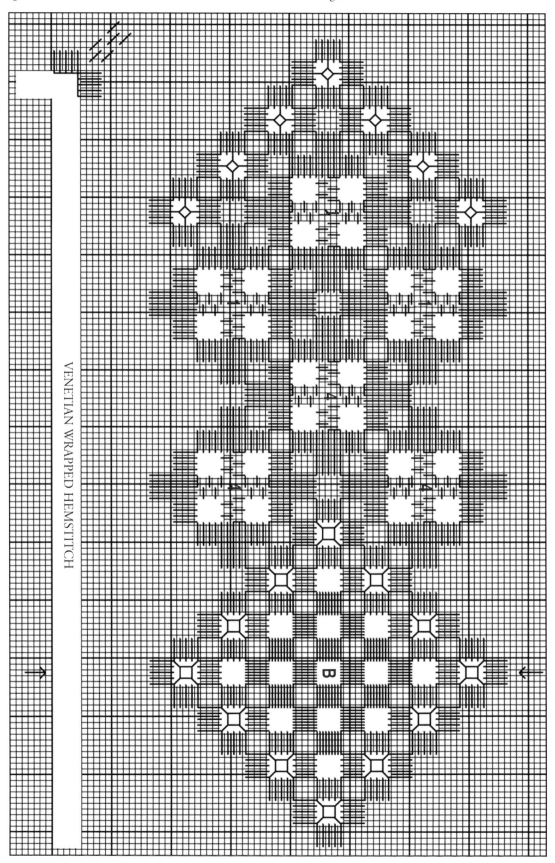

VENETIAN WRAPPED HEMSTITCH

Diagram 4 (blocks A, 2, 6)

This diagram shows half of the motif. The other half is its mirror image.

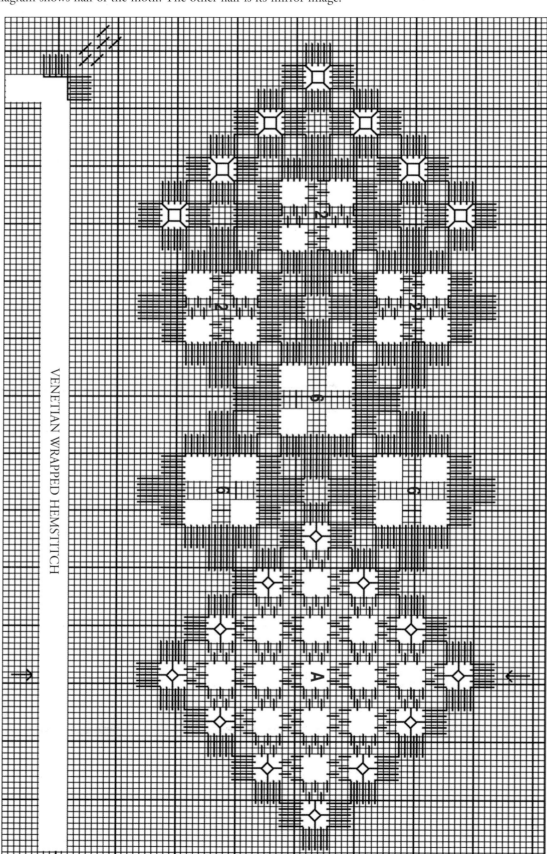

VENETIAN WRAPPED HEMSTITCH